Wels

LADIES IN R   ENT

LADIES IN RETIREMENT

Edward Percy and Reginald Denham

*The Authors dedicate this play to the
memory of the French prototypes
who wrote it with their lives.*

WARNER CHAPPELL PLAYS

LONDON

A Time Warner Company

This Warner Chappell Classics edition first published in 1993
by Warner Chappell Plays Ltd
129 Park Street, London W1Y 3FA

ISBN 0 85676 104 4

Printed by Commercial Colour Press, London E7

LADIES IN RETIREMENT was first presented at the St. James'
Theatre, London on 12th December, 1939, with the following
cast:

LUCY GILHAM	Joan Kemp-Welch
LEONORA FISKE	Mary Merrall
ELLEN CREED	Mary Clare
ALBERT FEATHER	Richard Newton
LOUISA CREED	Margaret Watson
EMILY CREED	Phyllis Morris
SISTER THERESA	Olga Slade

Produced by Reginald Denham

The play was presented at the Henry Miller Theatre, New
York, on 26th March, 1940, with the following cast:

LUCY GILHAM	Evelyn Ankers
LEONORA FISKE	Isobel Elsom
ELLEN CREED	Flora Robson
ALBERT FEATHER	Patrick O'Moore
LOUISA CREED	Estelle Winwood
EMILY CREED	Jessamine Newcombe
SISTER THERESA	Florence Edney

Produced by Reginald Denham

THE SETTING

The Scene is set in the living room of an old house on the
marshes of the Thames estuary, some ten miles to the east of
Gravesend.

ACT I

Scene One:	A June morning in 1885.
Scene Two:	An afternoon in the following September.
Scene Three:	Late afternoon, a week later.

ACT II

Scene One:	A Saturday night in mid-November.
Scene Two:	Sunday morning.

ACT III

Scene One:	The following Wednesday night.
Scene Two:	Thursday morning.

NOTE: This play is intended to be taken throughout at a
rapid tempo.

ACT ONE

Scene One

*Estuary House is an old pre-Tudor farmhouse situated below
the town of Gravesend in the Thames marshes made so
famous by Dickens in his "Great Expectations." It stands at a
small height above the level pastures which stretch out to the
massive stone walls bounding the great river.*

It belongs in this year 1885, to MISS LEONORA FISKE. MISS
FISKE *is an uncommon type. She is a retired lady of easy
virtue. She has had good friends - one or two of whom pay
her small quarterly allowances - and she has saved money.
She has chosen to spend the last years of her life in rural
retirement, and she occupies this lonely old house with her
friend and housekeeper-companion,* MISS ELLEN CREED.

*The living room has been made by throwing two or three
rooms together. It is, therefore, a large lofty room, with its
ceiling on different levels and this has the effect, when it is
evening and the room is only half-lighted, of dividing the
space into mountains and valleys of lights and shadows. A
pleasant enough room in daylight, but perhaps a little eerie
after dark.*

*Facing the audience is a huge, inset, open hearth of red brick
where, in winter, a fire of logs is burnt, at either end of
which is an old settle. In the chimney wall, between the settle
to stage right and the fire, is the iron door of a Kentish bake
oven. It is about two feet six inches square, and about the
same distance above the floor of the hearth. It has a ring
handle on the side nearest the centre of the hearth, and a
staple has been driven into the adjoining brickwork so that
the door can be, as it now is, fastened by a padlock passing
through both ring and staple.*

*In the hearth stands a long-handled implement of polished
steel with a spade-like termination once used for lifting
loaves out of such an oven when baked. This is technically
termed a "slice."*

*Stage right of the hearth is a fine old built-in dresser filled
with attractive crockery and brassware.*

*In the centre of the stage right wall is the front door opening
into the room, the hinge at the far side. It is an oak door with
a bronze knocker which can be seen when the door is opened.
On the side of this door furthest away is a latticed window.*

*In the back wall, stage left of the hearth, is an arched
doorway showing a flight of oak stairs leading up and
winding away out of sight round the chimney. The door opens
into the room and, when open, lies against the wall.*

*Halfway down the stage left wall is another door leading to
the kitchen and back premises of the house, opening
outwards.*

*The walls are of beam and old brick which is fast changing
from red to violet. The floor is stone flagged.*

The furniture is individual and rather important. MISS FISKE,
*like many "moderns" of her period, is a devotee of antiques
and bric-a-brac, and she has assembled together a motley
collection of household goods, all interesting if a little
baroque, but without any particular adherence to style or
method.*

*To the left, a small Early Victorian pianoforte. It is black and
is decorated with panels of pink and white rose bouquets
painted somewhat in the Dutch manner. On this stands a
large mandarin in porcelain with a nodding head. Centrally,
there is a round, highly polished, inlaid ormolu table, and,
round it and elsewhere in the room a set of several ormolu
chairs. To the right of the room stands a late Georgian sofa,
its head facing the downstage window. Behind the sofa is a
little occasional table covered with nick-knacks - among
them a silver sweetmeat box, full, at the moment, of sugar
plums, one or two little tortoise-shell and agate boxes and a
silver snuff box. Beyond that stands on Oriental gong. There
is a walnut bureau between the hearth and the staircase
archway. Beyond the door to the kitchen premises is a walnut
grandfather clock with a clear, penetrating bell-like strike.*

*Against the wall below this door is a half-moon mahogany
table on which stands a fair-sized statue of the Virgin in a
sky-blue robe carrying the Child. In front of the statue are*

*two little candles (not lighted) in little brass, "religious"
sticks, one or two devotional books and a rosary. In front of
this domestic altar is a prie-dieu.*

*In front of the dresser stands a grandfather chair. Above the
hearth is a long mantle crowded with blue Oriental and Delft
china in splendid confusion. There are some well-worn
Persian rugs on the stone floor.*

*It is a hot June morning. The sun is streaming in. The front
door and the windows are wide open. Through these you can
see a great expanse of blue sky which suggests that the house
stands slightly above the marshes.*

*The room is empty. From the distance comes the call of a
convent bell. It has rather a flat, ugly tone, and is more like
the tickling of a giant watch than a bell.*

LUCY GILHAM, *a pretty young maid, in a pink print dress and
white cap and apron of the period, comes down the staircase
carrying a carpet bag. She is rather a flighty type.* ELLEN
CREED'S *voice calls to her down the stairway from above. It is
an arresting voice, firm and clear.*

ELLEN'S VOICE   Look down the lane and see if Bates is
                coming.

LUCY   Yes, Miss. (*She crosses the room, sets down
                the bag by the front door and stepping outside
                looks along the lane. Then she returns and
                calls up the stairway.*) Yes, Miss! The trap's
                just passing the Priory now!

ELLEN'S VOICE   Where's Miss Fiske?

LUCY   I think she's in the wood lodge.

ELLEN'S VOICE   Tell her I shall be going in a minute.

                (LUCY *comes to the kitchen door, opens it and
                calls.*)

LUCY   Miss Fiske, Miss!

LEONORA'S   (*calling*) Yes! What is it?
VOICE

LUCY   Miss Creed's just off, Miss!

LEONORA'S   All right. I'm coming.
VOICE

                        (LEONORA FISKE *enters from the kitchen door.*
                        She is wearing gardener's gloves and carries
                        a small bunch of kingcups and a little brass
                        "religious" vase full of water. LEONORA *is*
                        elderly - sixty, perhaps - but she emulates all
                        the airs, graces and gaiety of youth. She is
                        active in her movements. She is carefully
                        rouged and enamelled, and wears a somewhat
                        obvious auburn wig, bright and curled and
                        scented. She is wearing a violet dress and a
                        green silk shawl. She is a good-hearted
                        woman with a shrewd sense of wit and a
                        rather quick temper. She is a Roman Catholic,
                        and - in spite of her career - genuinely
                        devoted to her faith.)

LEONORA   Is the trap here?

LUCY   Yes, Miss. It's just here.

                        (LEONORA *sets the bowl and flowers down on*
                        the table, removes her gloves, and begins to
                        arrange them.)

LEONORA   Miss Creed will have nice time for her train.
                        (*With a twinkle.*) We were almost wise,
                        weren't we, to order the trap half an hour
                        before she wanted it? (*Looking at the*
                        grandfather clock.) He's only twenty minutes
                        late.

LUCY   No two clocks agree in these parts.

LEONORA   That's the charm of the estuary. Nothing to
                        measure time by except the tides.

LUCY   And the bell at the Priory. But you can't rely
                        on that - because the nuns are always
                        oversleeping themselves.

LEONORA   You shouldn't say that about the Sisters,
           Lucy.

LUCY   A lot of old spinsters all herded up together
           with nothing to think about but their thoughts!
           It's against nature.

LEONORA   Tch! Tch! Tch!

LUCY   (*realising that she is being slightly tactless*)
           Oh - I'm sorry, Miss. I keep forgetting you're
           a Papist.

           (*There is the sound of a horse and trap
           drawing up outside.*)

LEONORA   Ah, here's Bates. Put Miss Creed's bag in the
           trap. And make sure the wooden flap's bolted.
           They won't want it to go rolling down the hill
           just when they've got to the top - like last
           time.

           (LUCY *takes the bag out of the front door.*
           LEONORA *follows her to the door.*)

           Oh, he's got the little chestnut cob that
           crosses it's legs! (*She hurries to the stairway
           and calls up.*) Ellen! It's time you were going.

           (*As she returns,* LUCY *re-enters the house
           carrying a pair of birds.*)

LUCY   Mr Bates has brought us some curlew. His boy
           shot 'em over on Cooling Marsh this morning.

LEONORA   I expect they'll want hanging.

LUCY   I'll go and put them in the dairy.

LEONORA   (*going out of the front door, speaking to*
           BATES) Thank you so much, Mr Bates. It is
           kind of you.

BATES' VOICE You're very welcome, Ma'am.

(ELLEN CREED *comes down the stairway. She is wearing a bonnet and cloak. She is a tall, striking-looking woman, rather younger than* LEONORA, *dark and plainly dressed. She has considerable dignity. Her eyes are very expressive and her features clear-cut. She would even be handsome if her lips were not so thin and compressed. The perfect housekeeper of the period, you would say at first glimpse. As she enters,* LUCY *has just reached the kitchen door.*)

ELLEN   What have you got there, Lucy?

LUCY   A couple of curlew - from Mr Bates.

(*She goes out through the kitchen door just as* LEONORA *enters from the front door, which she closes behind her. She comes to* ELLEN.)

LEONORA   I've just told Bates to stop at the brick kilns on the way. I've been counting those bricks in the yard. I believe they've sent me half a load short. And, look here, Ellen, there are a couple of things before you go. (*She crosses to the bureau and takes out a letter which she gives to* ELLEN.) I want you to take this letter to my lawyer. Mr Scott - Staple Inn. You did go there once before for me, didn't you?

ELLEN   Yes, it's by the old buildings in Holborn, isn't it?

LEONORA   Don't lose it. It's got some instructions in it about those Brazilian bonds of mine. I don't think they're as sound as they ought to be. I'm going to put the money into railways instead.

ELLEN   I think you're so brave, dear, the way you put your money into things. When I had money I was always afraid to let it out of my hands.

LEONORA   (*taking up the vase of kingcups, with a pleasantly superior smile*) But it got away somehow, didn't it?

ELLEN   I had so many mouths to feed.

                (LEONORA *takes the vase and places it before the Virgin. When she has done so she crosses herself.* ELLEN *watches this with a suggestion of disapproval.*)

LEONORA   You've certainly been a wonderful sister.

ELLEN   I've found a very kind friend.

LEONORA   Fiddle!

ELLEN   (*with deep feeling*) You can't tell what it means to me to be able to offer my sisters such a holiday. And it's so good of you to let me go up and fetch them. They'd never have faced the journey alone.

LEONORA   I'm quite looking forward to their visit. (*She takes a sugar-plum from the sweetmeat box and pops it into her mouth.*) You've talked so much about them. I feel they're old friends.

ELLEN   They're rather pathetic, you know, dear. But they're all I've got left.

LEONORA   (*who is not paying much attention, darting back to the bureau*) Oh, there's one other thing, Ellen.

ELLEN   What's that?

LEONORA   (*handing her a second letter*) I want you to call at this address. It's just off Berkeley Square - anyone will tell you. Go to the servant's entrance. Ask for Mr Blades - he's the butler. Say you've come from me with a note for Lord Kenardington. Will he give it to his lordship privately? And wait for an answer.

ELLEN   (*rather significantly*) What's the best time to call?

LEONORA   Let me see. Harry always used to dine at
           eight. Call at half past seven.

ELLEN   Very well, dear.

LEONORA   (*opening the front door*) And, whatever you
           do, don't lose the reply.

ELLEN   (*turning suddenly, in a quiet voice*) Hasn't it
           come this quarter?

LEONORA   No.

ELLEN   After all you've been spending, too! Oh, dear!

LEONORA   (*unwilling that* BATES *should hear anything of
           this*) Go along, Ellen, go along. Have a good
           journey.

           (ELLEN *goes out.* LEONORA *stands watching.
           The trap turns and rattles away.* LEONORA
           *waves. By now the convent bell has stopped.
           She comes back into the room.* LUCY *enters
           from the kitchen with a parcel.*)

LUCY   I've been in such a fuss this morning, what
           with Miss Creed getting off, I forgot to give
           you this. It came by the post. There was
           nothing else.

LEONORA   (*taking it and undoing it*) You really must try
           and not be so forgetful, Lucy.

           (LEONORA *opens the parcel. It contains a copy
           of the score of "The Mikado." She gives a
           little purr of pleasure.*)

           Oh! This is nice!

LUCY   (*inquisitively*) What's that, Miss?

LEONORA   It's the new comic opera. I used to tour the
           provinces with the gentleman who's sent it to
           me. Look, he's signed it for me - Rutland
           Barrington.

LUCY   (*reading the title*) "The Mick-a-doo" . . .

LEONORA   "The Mikado." It's been the rage of London
                for months. (*Giving* LUCY *the wrapper and
                string.*) Here, run along and take this paper
                and string. Now we've got this room
                comparatively straight, I want it kept straight.

                (LUCY *goes.* LEONORA *flutters excitedly to the
                piano, turns over the score at random, and
                then begins to play the song "Tit-Willow."
                You can see she is delighted with the music
                and the excuse for playing. As she is at the
                end of the verse a man's voice is heard
                outside beginning to sing the words.*)

VOICE   (*off*) "Though I probably shall not exclaim as
                I die, Oh, willow, tit-willow, tit-willow!"

                (LEONORA *stops playing in astonishment. A
                young man is standing in the sunny doorway.
                He is a little fellow of the type for which the
                word "cad" was coined. He is jaunty and
                impudent, and, in consequence, in great
                favour with the ladies. He has a bright
                lustrous eye and a little line of down low
                down on his upper lip. There is a touch of the
                Cockney about him especially in his over-
                dressiness. He wears a check cut-away coat
                and trousers, a brightly coloured, starched
                shirt with collar and cuffs to match and a
                wide-brimmed "boater" hat. He is a second-
                rate clerk and looks it. His name is* ALBERT
                FEATHER. LEONORA *rises.*)

ALBERT   Go on. Don't stop.

LEONORA   What are you doing here?

ALBERT   Listening.

LEONORA   (*instantly responding*) Well, either come in or
                go out.

                (*He comes in with a little chuckle.*)

ALBERT   I'm really looking for Miss Creed. She lives
            here, doesn't she?

LEONORA   Yes. She lives here. But she's just driven into
            Rochester, didn't you pass her on the road?

ALBERT   No. I've just walked over from Gravesend.
            Along the Thames wall and up through the
            saltings.

LEONORA   I wonder you found your way. They're tricky
            - the marshes, you know.

ALBERT   Don't I half? I've been up to my knees in
            three jolly dykes already.

LEONORA   Hadn't you better sit down?

ALBERT   Thanks - if I shan't damage the furniture.
            How long shall I have to wait for my aunt?

LEONORA   (*in surprise*) Your aunt? You're not Albert,
            are you?

ALBERT   Albert Feather. That's me.

LEONORA   The one who works in a bank at Gravesend?

ALBERT   Did work. Yes. (*Feeling this needs some
            explanation.*) That's rather what I've come to
            see Aunt Ellen about. I must get back tonight
            though. How long shall I have to wait for her?

LEONORA   (*blandly, helping herself to another sugar-
            plum*) About a week, I think.

ALBERT   (*staggered*) A week?

LEONORA   Yes. She's gone to London.

ALBERT   (*with something like despair in his voice*) By
            Jove! That's done it. That *has* done it.

LEONORA   What's the matter? Can't I help?

ALBERT	But I don't know who you are - or what you're doing in my aunt's house.
LEONORA	Who told you it was your aunt's house?
ALBERT	Well, isn't it? Aunt Ellen wrote she was living here. Aunt Ellen's a great one for keeping up with the family. You aren't a lost cousin from Australia, by any chance?
LEONORA	No. We're not related, Albert. If you want to know, Estuary House is *my* house, and your aunt's living with me - as my housekeeper-companion.
ALBERT	Well, I'm blowed. The artful old geezer! She *has* led the family up the garden path.
LEONORA	Well, don't say anything about it. I dare say it's a sense of false pride, you know. We all suffer from it. You see, the poor dear's lost most of her little bit of money. I expect she doesn't want you to know she's come down in the world.
ALBERT	(*rather eagerly*) Has she lost everything?
LEONORA	Practically.
ALBERT	What happened to the old curio shop in Bartholomew Close? I thought that was a little gold mine.
LEONORA	I'm afraid more gold went into it than ever came out. That happens to a lot of gold mines.
ALBERT	(*pondering*) I say - this *is* a blow.
LEONORA	I used to buy things at her shop. I'm very interested in bric-à-brac. If you use your eyes, you'll see quite a lot of Bartholomew Close about the room now.
ALBERT	(*looking round*) Well, well! So there is, now you mention it. (*He is beside the piano now*

and notices the mandarin.) Why, if it isn't the
old Grand Cham himself! He came out of the
old place, I know.

LEONORA   Yes.

ALBERT   I used to play with him when I was a kid.
Does his head still nod? (*He touches it and
the figure responds.*) So it does!

LEONORA   I bought him there three years ago. He was
the beginning of our association. Then, when
I saw she wasn't doing well and I was leaving
London, I asked her if she'd like to come with
me.

ALBERT   I expect you've been awfully good to her.

LEONORA   Oh, I don't know. She suits me. Besides,
we've got this mutual taste in antiques.
Getting this place right has been a great
interest. Would you believe it? The farmers
who had this before had matchboarded in
these walls, and then wallpapered the
matchboarding with terra-cotta roses!

ALBERT   You must have had an army of workmen here.

LEONORA   Workmen? Good gracious, no. (*She takes
another sugar-plum.*) We did it ourselves.

ALBERT   (*in amazement*) What? You and Aunt Ellen?

LEONORA   It's not so difficult - if you've got plenty of
time. Your aunt's very clever with her hands.
And we don't hurry ourselves. Time doesn't
matter here, you know.

ALBERT   Well, you're lucky. Time's everything to me -
just at the moment. If it's not asking . . .
what's your name?

LEONORA   I'm Miss Fiske. Leonora Fiske.

ALBERT   (*a little doubtfully*) I wonder if *you* could help me.

LEONORA   I don't know till you tell me.

ALBERT   (*putting his fingers into his collar and easing his neck*) Well, I - I hardly like to tell you.

LEONORA   (*with humour*) I see. What's the amount?

ALBERT   (*after a moment*) Twelve pounds.

LEONORA   (*a little startled, as she has envisaged a "fiver".*) My goodness! That's a lot of money. And what do you want twelve pounds for, Albert?

ALBERT   I need it for a debt.

LEONORA   Won't it wait?

ALBERT   No. I must have it by tonight.

LEONORA   Why is it so urgent?

ALBERT   (*pauses, then out it comes*) I'm short in my account at the bank. Petty cash.

LEONORA   (*her eyes widening*) I see. That is serious isn't it?

ALBERT   I've got till tomorrow to put it back - when the cashier checks up. (*He shows something of what he has been going through.*) It means jug, if they find out. (*With naivete.*) I'm sure Aunt Ellen'll pay you back.

LEONORA   (*kind but firm*) I think we'd better leave Aunt Ellen out of it. What have you been spending the money on? Cards? Racing?

ALBERT   (*he pauses again*) No. A girl.

LEONORA   Are you engaged to her?

ALBERT   No. She's not that sort.

LEONORA   (*expressively*) Ah, the other kind. I know.

ALBERT   She's an actress. There was a company at Gravesend last week.

LEONORA	(*with interest*) At the old Grand?
ALBERT	(*seeing her interest*) Do you know it?
LEONORA	I've played there. Years ago, of course.
ALBERT	You weren't an actress, were you?
LEONORA	(*chuckling*) Front row of the chorus. Fourth from the right.
ALBERT	Funny! She's in the chorus, too. But you've moved up in life.
LEONORA	Perhaps I've been lucky. I suppose you took her out to supper. And then she persuaded you to go round the shops with her.
ALBERT	How do you know?
LEONORA	Imagination, Albert. She may even have let you kiss her. And I'm quite sure she promised you a great deal more.
ALBERT	(*viciously*) The little cheat!
LEONORA	Oh, she probably has her point of view.
ALBERT	Anyway, she's over the hills now to some other town where I suppose she'll find some other fool to steal for her.
LEONORA	(*perhaps he has touched her on the raw*) Very well, Albert. You shall have your twelve pounds. After all, I owe it to you - in a sense. Or to some other fool.
	(*To her surprise he breaks down. It is half genuine relief, half the snivelling of the natural beggar.*)
	Oh, my goodness! Don't do that.
ALBERT	(*wiping his eyes*) It's only that I'm so grateful.
LEONORA	It's no earthly use being hysterical about money, Albert.

ALBERT	(*looking up at her, slyly*) Do you mean that? You're hard as nails really, aren't you?
LEONORA	No. But I'm not going to burst into tears about somebody else's twelve pounds. The scrape's over. You're out of it.
ALBERT	I wish I knew how to thank you.
LEONORA	(*with a change of tone*) You're not in a violent hurry, are you?
ALBERT	(*wondering what is coming*) No, not now, ma'am.
LEONORA	Tell me something about your family - about your aunts. Not Aunt Ellen. The others. Aunt Louisa and Aunt Emily.
ALBERT	Oh! You mean the potty ones?
LEONORA	(*this time it is her turn to be surprised*) Potty?
ALBERT	Well, odd, perhaps I should say. They're quite harmless.
LEONORA	That's a comfort. They're coming to stay here. That's why Aunt Ellen's on her way to London now. She's gone to fetch them.
ALBERT	Coming to stay here? I wish you joy! They're not quite your style, are they?
LEONORA	I don't know. I've never seen them.
ALBERT	Oh, haven't you? Then you've got a good time coming. (*Realising from her face that he may have gone too far.*) Of course, you may be able to handle 'em. I dare say you'll rub along all right.
LEONORA	They seem to mean a great deal to your Aunt Ellen.

ALBERT   Oh, well, they would. They've sort of taken
                the place of children with her. Somehow,
                when she's with Aunt Louisa and Aunt Emily
                she always makes me think of a tigress with
                her cubs.

LEONORA   (*laughing*) Ellen? A tigress? You silly boy. Is
                your mother alive?

ALBERT   No. She's been dead a long time. Aunt Ellen
                brought me up. (*With a change of tone.*) Well,
                I suppose I ought to be getting back - if
                you're really going to . . . to . . .

LEONORA   (*with humour*) Cough up the needful?

                (*They both laugh.*)

                I'll just run up and get my keys.

ALBERT   (*as she goes to the stairway*) You are a
                lifesaver, Miss Fiske. Pity there aren't more
                like you.

LEONORA   (*a little grimly*) That's a matter of opinion,
                Albert.

ALBERT   Mind if I have a tinkle on your ivories? I
                never get a chance on a piano like this. We've
                only got an old tin kettle where I lodge.

LEONORA   No. Do.

                (*She hurries upstairs.* ALBERT *looks round for
                a moment. Then the pocket Autolycus in him
                draws him to the table of nick-knacks. He
                picks up the silver snuff box and slips it
                quietly into his pocket. Then he hurriedly sits
                himself at the piano. He begins to play and
                sing, in a half-voice, "The Man on the Flying
                Trapeze."* LUCY *enters wonderingly from the
                kitchen. Discovering* ALBERT, *she gapes. He
                turns his head and sees her.*)

ALBERT   Hullo!

LUCY	You did scare me! I thought I was hearing things.
ALBERT	You were.
LUCY	(*rather coyly*) But I mean - a man's voice. (*She giggles.*) So funny - here!
ALBERT	(*becoming at once the cheap "accapareur de femmes"*) Doesn't the tide wash up many male fish, my angel?
LUCY	No. Men's as scarce here as hansom cabs. We're a covey of old women. There's only the nuns down at the Priory and us.
ALBERT	What about the butcher, the baker and the candlestick maker? Don't they call?
LUCY	Oh, yes. But they're all old. Everybody's old on the marsh. The young 'uns go off to London or to foreign parts. Soon as they can.
ALBERT	Are you going off to foreign parts?
LUCY	Depends.
ALBERT	Depends? On what?
LUCY	If anyone ever asks me.
ALBERT	I shouldn't think with eyes like them there'd be any difficulty.
LUCY	(*coquetting him*) Oh, go on!
ALBERT	What's your name?
LUCY	Lucy.
ALBERT	You don't come from the marshes, do you?
LUCY	My mother lives in Isle of Grain. I went out to service first in Chatham.
ALBERT	Oh? Quite a town bird - like me!

LUCY	Who are you?
ALBERT	I'm Albert. Miss Creed's nephew.
LUCY	Funny - I've never heard about you.
ALBERT	That must be remedied. How about making the most of a male fish, now one has been washed up? What about a smacker?
	(*He puts his arm around her and tries to kiss her, but she draws away, eyeing him covertly.*)
LUCY	No. You mustn't. I don't know you.
ALBERT	But you don't have to know people to kiss them!
LUCY	I do.
ALBERT	(*with a shrug*) All right, my girl. It's your loss.
LUCY	(*going to the kitchen door with a hoity-toity air*) You do think a lot of yourself, don't you?
	(*There is a sound on the stairs and she flashes out just as* LEONORA *appears. The old lady looks very knowing.*)
LEONORA	Has Lucy been entertaining you, Albert?
ALBERT	(*nonchalantly*) She came in. We had a word or two.
LEONORA	Nice looker, isn't she?
ALBERT	I didn't notice.
LEONORA	Come, Albert. Don't lose your sense of humour. I hope you're not one of those people who won't learn from experience. Otherwise my twelve pounds may be rather wasted.
ALBERT	Don't you worry, Miss Fiske. I've had my lesson.
LEONORA	I hope so. (*She goes to the hearth and unlocks the bake-oven door.*) This is where we keep

our hoard. (*She opens the door and you see a large dark cavity in the brick work behind. She takes out a big, old-fashioned cash box.*) It's an old bake-oven really.

ALBERT   (*peering in with a whistle of astonishment*) Proper tomb, isn't it?

LEONORA   Yes. It runs the full width of the chimney. This is called a "slice." It's what they used to draw the loaves out with. Look.

(*She takes up the "slice" and plunges it into the aperture which swallows it right up to the handle. Then she withdraws it and stands it again in the hearth.*)

Of course, we don't use it as a bake-oven. It hasn't been used for years. When I came here I found this whole hearth walled up. With a hideous little gimcrack mantlepiece and a cast-iron grate!

ALBERT   That was worth uncovering, wasn't it!

LEONORA   (*at the table, opening the cash box*) Now then, Albert - twelve pounds, I think you said?

(*She takes out a little chamois leather bag full of gold and counts out twelve sovereigns.*)

ALBERT   I suppose you couldn't make it fifteen?

LEONORA   (*very directly*) No, I couldn't, Albert.

(*She hands him the money, replaces the bag, locks the cash box and puts it back in the oven, closing the door and locking the padlock.*)

ALBERT   Do I - do I give you an IOU?

LEONORA   No, thank you, Albert. This isn't a loan. I shouldn't like you to incur the remorse of not paying it back.

ALBERT   Do you mean that? I say! You're a trump. I'll
            never forget your kindness.

            (*He takes her hand and kisses it.*)

LEONORA   (*rather intrigued, laughing*) Very prettily
            done, Albert. (*She slaps his face playfully.*)
            There! Now let's forget all about it. (*By now
            she is ready to be rid of her visitor.*) I'm sorry
            I can't offer you lunch.

ALBERT   Oh, I'll be able to get something at one of the
            farms on the way back. After all, what's one
            lunch compared to bread and skelly for a
            couple of years?

LEONORA   And I shan't mention your call to Aunt Ellen.

ALBERT   I'd be very grateful if you wouldn't. Er, what
            about the girl?

LEONORA   I'll see to that, too. Goodbye, Albert.

ALBERT   Goodbye, Miss Fiske. And I'll never forget
            your kindness as long as I live.

LEONORA   Oh, I hope you'll live much longer than that.

            (*He has taken up his hat. He smiles, bows and
            goes jauntily.* LEONORA *stands looking after
            him. She, too, smiles - a little twisted,
            perhaps. He is young, he has a way with him,
            he is probably a rogue, but - he is a man!
            Then she hurries to the kitchen door and
            calls: "Lucy! I want you!" She returns to the
            piano and sits as if to resume her playing.*
            LUCY *enters.*)

            Lucy, you met the young gentleman who's
            just gone, didn't you?

LUCY   Yes, Miss.

LEONORA   Did you like him?

LUCY   I thought he was a very affable young
            gentleman, Miss.

LEONORA   Yes. I think that's a very good description of
               him. Though "plausible" might be better. He's
               been in a little trouble. And I've helped him.
               I don't want to worry Miss Creed about it. So
               we'd better not say he's been here. Do you
               understand?

LUCY   Yes, Miss.

LEONORA   That's all. Thank you, Lucy.

               (LUCY *retires.* LEONORA *resumes her playing of*
               "Tit-Willow." The lights fade.)

Scene Two

An afternoon in the following September. At the window a
little elderly woman is standing. She is gazing out of the open
casement across the marshes through a large nautical
telescope. She is dressed in a worn, wide-skirted garment of
rust-coloured velvet, many years out of date. She is a thin,
faded, shadowy personality, simple rather as a child is
simple, fluttering, fretful, futile. At times, though, there is
something decidedly comical about her. This is LOUISA CREED.
A knitted shawl and a large workbag lie on the armchair
behind her. There is a brief pause. Then ELLEN *enters from*
the kitchen.

ELLEN   You oughtn't to be standing by that window,
               darling. The wind's turning quite cold.

LOUISA   (*rather fearfully*) Don't be cross with me,
               Ellen. I'm so happy, looking.

ELLEN   (*taking up* LOUISA'S *shawl and arranging it*
               tenderly around her shoulders) Well, put your
               shawl on, then.

LOUISA   Oh, but I'm strong. Much stronger than when
               I came. (*Looking through the telescope.*) It
               must be quite rough on the river. Do you see
               the waves? They're like little white feathers
               blowing about.

ELLEN	Is that Emily coming over the marsh?
LOUISA	(*altering the direction of the telescope*) Yes. Her apron's loaded. I wonder what she's picked up this time. Oh, Ellen! Isn't it exciting? She brings in such pretty things. I wish I were brave like Emily. I should like to take long walks, too, and pick up things and bring them home. Perhaps I shall be able to when I've stayed here longer.
ELLEN	I'm sure you will, darling.
LOUISA	(*anxiously*) I shall be staying here, shan't I? You're not planning to send me away, are you, Ellen?
ELLEN	No, of course I'm not.
LOUISA	This is what you always promised us. A little house in the country and the three of us being in it together. You and Emily and me.
ELLEN	Yes, dear. that's the one thing I've schemed for ever since we had to give up the old house.
LOUISA	I wonder who's living there now. I often think of the rhododendron hedge and the flag irises down by the river. And our copper beech tree! Do you remember how we three planted it, Ellen - with Father looking on and laughing at us?
ELLEN	I expect Richmond's changed - like everything else.
LOUISA	Of course this could never be like Richmond! But it's nice here.
ELLEN	And Miss Fiske's been very kind to us.
LOUISA	(*clouding*) Miss Fiske . . . may I tell you something, Ellen? Just one of my secrets?

ELLEN   Of course, darling.

LOUISA   I don't like Miss Fiske. I don't like her
             religion. Can't we send her away? Then it
             would be really just the three of us.

ELLEN   But I keep telling you, Louisa - it's her house.

LOUISA   (*shaking her head*) Oh, no. You'll never make
             me believe that. You've always had your own
             house. This is yours. Here are your things.
             You've always had your own house, Ellen,
             haven't you? You're the clever one. And
             you'll always keep me near you, won't you? I
             don't want to be sent back to Kennington. To
             those awful ugly streets. Nothing to look at
             from the window.

ELLEN   Darling, I've promised you I won't send you back.

LOUISA   I think Miss Fiske wants me to go. She wants
             us both to go - Emily and me. I think so.

ELLEN   You're just imagining it.

LOUISA   No, I'm not, Ellen. I'm not imagining it.

ELLEN   But, darling, I'm sure I can persuade her to
             let you stay.

LOUISA   Yes, Ellen. I'm sure you can. You can do
             anything. (*She has wandered across the room
             and stands looking at the statue of the Virgin
             with wondering disapproval.*) I wish you'd
             take this away. It isn't right to worship idols,
             is it?

ELLEN   We can't take it away. It doesn't belong to us.

LOUISA   Father always said that Roman Catholics
             aren't saved. I don't trust people who aren't
             saved.

             (*The front door opens and* LEONORA *sails in.
             She is carrying a basket of ripe William*

pears. This time she is dressed in a bright blue gown. She is kind and charming to her guests, but you can see that they have begun to get badly on her nerves.)

LEONORA   (*brightly*) I've just been down to the Priory. Look what the Reverend Mother's given me.

ELLEN   Oh, what lovely pears! Look, Louisa.

LEONORA   Yes. They're Williams. Have one, dear.

ELLEN   (*taking one*) May I?

LEONORA   Won't you have one, Miss Louisa?

LOUISA   Did you say they came from the convent?

LEONORA   Yes.

LOUISA   (*shrinking a little*) Oh I don't think I . . .

ELLEN   (*almost a command*) Do, dear.

LOUISA   (*taking one*) Thank you. May I eat it later?

LEONORA   Of course.

ELLEN   (*as though to cover* LOUISA'S *ungraciousness*) I think I'll keep mine till supper, too.

LEONORA   (*sitting at the table*) Well, I'm going to eat one now.

(ELLEN *goes to the dresser and fetches a dessert plate and silver knife and fork which she sets before* LEONORA. *She has laid her own and* LOUISA'S *pear on a plate on the dresser.*)

ELLEN   They're beautiful pears.

LEONORA   They're from that tree by the pond.

ELLEN   The one that looks so lovely in the spring?

LEONORA   Yes.

LOUISA   (*almost clapping her hands*) Oh, I shall like to see that.

LEONORA   (*dryly*) I wish you could. What have you been
           doing all today?

LOUISA   I've been resting. And looking at things.

ELLEN   She's been watching the sailing barges going
           up and down the Thames.

LOUISA   There've been some big steamers passing,
           too. It's been the turn of the tide. They've
           been going up and down. I do think people are
           brave to go on the water in boats.

LEONORA   (*beginning on the pear*) It doesn't strike me as
           particularly brave. No braver than living in a
           city where you might be run over or have a
           chimney pot blow down on your head.

LOUISA   But I don't like living in a city. Just for that
           reason. And I don't care to go out. I'm not
           very brave. I don't go out in the streets.
           That's why I like being here. It's so lovely -
           so safe.

LEONORA   I don't know what you'll do when you go
           back to London, then!

LOUISA   (*like a sly child*) Ah, but I'm not going back
           to London.

LEONORA   Aren't you?

ELLEN   That's just Louisa's way of telling you how
           much she's enjoying it here.

LOUISA   Yes. I am enjoying it.

ELLEN   That telescope's been such a pleasure to her.
           She's never had much opportunity of using it
           before.

           (LOUISA *fetches her telescope and exhibits it
           to* LEONORA *while she eats.* LEONORA *eyes it
           with no particular pleasure.*)

LOUISA   Yes. It's a beautiful instrument, isn't it? I
             keep it beautifully polished don't I? It
             belonged to the man I was going to marry. He
             was the captain of a sailing ship. It was lost
             in a typhoon in the Indian Ocean. They were
             sailing from Madagascar with a cargo of
             raffia grass. You know, it's the thing they tie
             up plants with in gardens! Fancy a boat load
             of something you tie up plants with in
             gardens! Funny, isn't it? They were all
             drowned. He hadn't taken this with him on his
             last voyage. His sister gave it me. I've kept it
             ever since.

LEONORA   Oh, dear! What a tragic story!

LOUISA   It doesn't seem tragic to me now. You see,
             I've no picture of him, and it's so long ago
             I've almost forgotten what he looked like.

             (*She takes the telescope back to the window.*
             LEONORA *rises, thankful to escape.*)

LEONORA   How sticky these pears make one! I must go
             and dip my fingers.

             (*She goes out through the kitchen door.*
             LOUISA *picks up her workbag and slips the two
             pears* LEONORA *gave them into it.*)

ELLEN   (*sharply*) What are you doing? You mustn't
             do that!

LOUISA   (*in a whisper*) I'll burn them. Before I go up
             to bed. In the stove in the kitchen. I'll slip in
             when no one's there.

ELLEN   Give them to me at once.

LOUISA   (*handing them over like a naughty child*) You
             mustn't be cross with me, Ellen. They come
             from the nuns.

ELLEN   (*putting them back on the dresser*) The nuns
             didn't make the tree, Louisa.

LOUISA   No. I suppose they didn't. I see. (*Nodding.*) Yes. Yes, I was wrong.

(EMILY CREED *enters from the front door. She is a big-boned elderly woman of a gipsy type. She, like* LOUISA, *is simple and has the same sense of dependence, but, in her case, she hates her inability to fend for herself, and is often sullen and resentful. She is wearing an old fashioned dark dress, the overskirt of which has been pinned up under an apron of dark blue cloth. The underskirt is stained with mud. Her apron, which she holds up basket-fashion, contains pieces of driftwood, a red cotton handkerchief full of shells, some seaweed and a dead bird. Her hair has been blown wild by the wind.*)

EMILY   Oh, dear. I am tired. I've walked miles. (*She kneels on the floor and lets the contents of her apron out upon it.*) That's the worst of the river. It leads you on. You always want to go round the next bend, and forget you've got to come all the way back.

ELLEN   What have you found this time, darling?

EMILY   Just driftwood. There's such a lot. But it's so heavy to carry. One wants an extra pair of arms.

ELLEN   You shouldn't tire yourself like this.

EMILY   Oh, but I enjoy it. I feel I must tidy up the river banks. But it's no good. Every tide washes up something fresh.

ELLEN   (*smiling*) I'm afraid you've set yourself a labour of Hercules.

EMILY   Oh, I knew you'd laugh. You always do. I know it's silly. But I hate waste. And I have done something for my board and lodging, haven't I? Look at the stack of wood I've collected out there for you, Ellen.

ELLEN	Yes, and I'm sure Miss Fiske's very grateful.
EMILY	Is she? She's never said anything. Not that I want any thanks.
	(She takes the handkerchief with the shells and the seaweed and the dead bird and lays them on the table.)
LOUISA	Why should she thank you, Emily? It's Ellen who should thank you. It's Ellen's house.
ELLEN	Louisa can't get it into her head that this house doesn't belong to me.
EMILY	*(emptying the shells on to the table)* But she's right in a way, isn't she? After all, Miss Fiske's quite dependent on you. Just as we are. She needs you. Just as we do.
ELLEN	That doesn't mean that her property belongs to me.
EMILY	I expect it will some day. She'll leave it to you. You'll see!
LOUISA	What pretty shells!
EMILY	Yes. I thought they'd be so useful. We can stick them on to boxes in patterns. You had one, d'you remember, Ellen, in you curiosity shop?
LOUISA	Oh look, Ellen. A dead bird.
EMILY	Yes. I found it. I showed it to a shepherd. He said it was a sea swallow. That it was only just dead. It was lying on this seaweed. Isn't it a lovely thing?
	(LEONORA enters. She stands transfixed before the litter on the floor.)
LEONORA	Oh, my goodness! More wood?

EMILY	Yes. I got a nice lot today. I shan't be satisfied till I've stocked you with wood for the winter.
LEONORA	Well, it's very nice of you, Miss Emily, but I do wish you'd take it round to the back door. It makes such a mess in here.
LOUISA	Emily wanted to show us what she's found. Besides she was very tired.
ELLEN	Don't worry about it, Leonora. I'll clear it up.

(She kneels down and proceeds to gather up the wood.)

LOUISA	*(fluttering round her)* No, Ellen. You mustn't be put to any trouble. It's our fault. Miss Fiske, don't you think we might ask for the maid?
EMILY	*(joining them)* No, it's my business. After all, I've carried it for more than a mile across the marsh.
ELLEN	Emily, go and sit down. You're tired.
LOUISA	No, Ellen. You do far too much as it is. Put it down, Ellen.

(As a result of their assistance the wood falls to the floor again.)

LEONORA	Well, I don't think we need have a tug of war about it. We'll adopt Miss Louisa's suggestion about the maid, shall we? *(Calling.)* Lucy!
LOUISA	My sister's not as strong as she thinks. And she's always doing things for other people.

(LUCY enters.)

LEONORA	Take that wood through into the shed, please, Lucy.

LUCY   There's no room in the shed, Miss. That's
            chock-full.

LEONORA   Well, I don't know what we're to do with it.

LUCY   I'll make a pile in the corner of the scullery here.

LEONORA   Very well. And bring Miss Emily a dustpan
            and brush. (*Sub-acidly.*) I think we should all
            clean up our messes, don't you?

EMILY   That's what I wanted to do before Ellen
            started interfering.

LOUISA   Oh, it wasn't Ellen, dear. It was me. It was
            my fault.

LEONORA   Well, don't start that all over again. (*To
            LUCY, who has gathered up the offending
            wood.*) And don't stand about, Lucy. Hurry up
            and fetch that dustpan.

LUCY   Yes, Miss. I was only listening.

            (*She goes.* LEONORA *suddenly sees the shells
            scattered on the table.*)

LEONORA   Oh, really, Ellen! This is too bad! My best
            polished table! Couldn't you have found a
            cloth?

ELLEN   I'm sorry. I ought to have remembered.

EMILY   Yes, you should have told me, Ellen. I'd no
            idea that table couldn't have things put on it.

LEONORA   But surely your common sense would tell you
            that shells will scratch a highly polished table!

EMILY   I didn't think.

            (*LUCY enters with the dustpan and brush. She
            stands by the kitchen door, keenly interested
            in the little domestic disturbance.*)

LEONORA	And what's this? Wet seaweed and a horrid dead bird! Ellen, really!
LOUISA	It's nothing to do with Ellen.
LEONORA	But, Miss Louisa, Ellen's responsible to me! No one knows better than she does how carefully an old piece must be handled. It'll take a month's hard polishing to put this right.
ELLEN	I'll put it right.
LOUISA	No. You shan't, Ellen. Let me do it. Let me. I'll polish it every day all through the winter.
LEONORA	That's very kind of you, Miss Louisa. But I'm afraid you won't be here all through the winter.
LOUISA	Oh, but we shall! We shall. Ellen says so.
ELLEN	You've made a mistake, Louisa. I said nothing of the kind.
LOUISA	But you did. You promised.
ELLEN	(*again the sense of command*) Louisa!
EMILY	(*her voice quivering with emotion*) Oh, please don't bully poor Louisa because of me, Ellen. And please don't be cross with Ellen, Miss Fiske. I brought in the shells and the sea bird. I picked them up. They're my treasures. They're quite harmless. They've given my sisters and me a great deal of pleasure. I know it's very simple of us. But we are simple. We don't understand expensive things because it's so long since we lived amongst them. (*Weeping.*) However, I see that my humble little finds are only starting a quarrel so they'd better be taken away. (*With a great scraping and clatter she sweeps all the shells and objects from the table into her apron, and goes upstairs sobbing bitterly.*

There is a brief pause. Then LEONORA, *almost beside herself, sees* LUCY.)

LEONORA   Oh, are you there, Lucy? Give me that. (*She takes the dustpan and brush, stoops and, in silence, sweeps up the litter from the floor. Then she hands them to* LUCY.) Thank you. Now get on with the supper.

(LUCY *goes.*)

LOUISA   I think I'd better go up to Emily, Ellen. I can hear her crying.

ELLEN   (*almost curtly*) No. Let her be. Go up to your own room, if you like. But don't disturb Emily.

(LOUISA, *after grimacing and putting out her tongue like a gamine at* LEONORA'S *back, scurries upstairs, shutting the door at the foot after her.*)

LEONORA   I'm sorry I was so put out, Ellen. But there's a limit to patience, you know.

ELLEN   It's I who should have apologised.

LEONORA   Nonsense, dear. I mustn't expect you to be responsible for your sisters.

ELLEN   But I *am* responsible for them.

LEONORA   I don't want to add to your troubles, and I know what a burden they are, but . . .

ELLEN   Oh, but, Leonora, they're no burden at all. When my father was dying he made them over to me. They're a sacred trust - just as if they were my children. I've always looked after them. I've supported them. Every penny I earn goes to them.

LEONORA   My dear, you must be either a saint or a fool!

ELLEN   But what would become of them if I didn't? You see, when I had the shop and it failed, I lost their little money as well as my own. Everything they have is invested in me, and I must give them *some* dividend.

LEONORA   Yes, but you must show a sense of proportion in dealing with them. For one thing, they're - well, they're not quite normal, are they?

ELLEN   Oh, I know they're simple-minded, but they're not mad. They're not insane. They've just never grown up properly.

LEONORA   Oh, I daresay they're harmless. At least I hope so. But you're forgetting that *I* haven't been brought up with them. They haven't been made over to *me*. And, while *you* may be used to them, *I* find them impossible to have about the house.

ELLEN   They *have* been a little naughty today, I admit. But I'll give them a good talking to, and then everything will be all right.

LEONORA   (*firmly*) That won't do, Ellen. I'm trying to tell you, as kindly as I can, that they've got to go.

ELLEN   (*she seems stunned*) To go? When? (*There is a pause.*) When do you want them to go?

LEONORA   At once. This week. I can't stand them any longer. I'm at the end of my tether.

ELLEN   I don't know how I shall break it to them.

LEONORA   (*growing exasperated*) But, my dear Ellen, I only invited them here for a few weeks. Didn't they understand that? They've been here nearly four months.

ELLEN   Oh, no! Surely not as long as that?

LEONORA   They came at the beginning of June, and now we're well into September. And another thing. I don't think you've been quite fair to me.

You never told me they were, well, what they are.

ELLEN   I told you they were rather pathetic.

LEONORA Yes, my dear. But pathetic's not next door to insane.

ELLEN   (*almost savagely*) They're not insane!

LEONORA Naturally, you put the best side of the picture forward. They're your own flesh and blood. But, insane or pathetic or whatever you choose to call them, they've overstayed their welcome. I won't have them here any longer.

ELLEN   It's your house, I know. But you'll have to give me a little time.

LEONORA What's time got to do with it?

ELLEN   Well, I don't quite know where I'll be able to send them.

LEONORA But surely they've only got to get into a train and go back where they came from?

ELLEN   No. I didn't keep on their room.

LEONORA But, my dear! You knew they weren't coming here on a visit for life!

ELLEN   I didn't want the expense. Besides, I hoped that perhaps you might have taken to them more than you have. I hoped we might be able to arrange something. It's a large house. There are several empty rooms. I was going to suggest that I should pay you something out of my wages towards their keep.

LEONORA Oh, you were, were you? And is that why Louisa made that odd remark just now?

ELLEN   What odd remark?

LEONORA That you'd promised her she should stay through the winter!

ELLEN   I never promised her.

LEONORA   I suspected something of the sort at the time.

ELLEN   I said I never promised her.

LEONORA   Very well. I accept that.

ELLEN   I admit I didn't realise quite how you felt. You've never an inkling of it.

LEONORA   My dear Ellen, are you quite blind? You must have seen that I've got more and more exasperated.

ELLEN   I thought we might have gone on as we were for a little longer.

LEONORA   Well, you know how I feel now. I hope you realise we can't. This little holiday has come to an end.

ELLEN   You make me feel my position very much. I suppose you want me to go, too?

LEONORA   My dear Ellen, of course not! We got on like a house on fire before they came. I don't regard you, dear, as my servant. I think of you as my friend. You know my pillar-to-post career hasn't made me any permanent ones. Mine's a lonely existence. Terribly lonely. It's bound to be. And I've no family - no relations to fall back on. Why, if I were to disappear tomorrow no one would be any the wiser! I shouldn't make a ripple on the surface. So, you see, I value your companionship. More, perhaps, than you realise. I definitely don't want you to go.

ELLEN   I'm afraid it won't be altogether easy to forget what you think about my sisters. Or that you turned them out when they were so happy.

LEONORA	But I haven't turned them out! Their visit's just come to its end in the normal way. That's all.
ELLEN	Things can never be quite the same, can they?
LEONORA	Ellen! Don't tell me that you're crazy, too! For goodness sake, try to see this thing sensibly. Don't you realise that you're being frightfully unreasonable?
ELLEN	(*sitting on the sofa*) People who've got all they want never understand how much the smallest thing means to those who haven't.
LEONORA	(*getting very angry*) Really! I don't think this calls for a sermon on charity! I've been more than generous to you and your sisters.
ELLEN	But it's a little cruel to give with one hand only to take away with the other.
LEONORA	Oh, my goodness! You're beginning to make me wish I'd never given at all!
ELLEN	People have always been very generous to you, Leonora. You've got a home. You've got investments. You've got your one or two - allowances, haven't you?
LEONORA	Well, what of it?
ELLEN	My sisters and I - we haven't any gentlemen to send us money.
LEONORA	That's hardly my fault, is it?
ELLEN	No, but don't you ever feel that you have a special responsibility to women like us?
LEONORA	I don't know what you're talking about!
ELLEN	Don't you owe a debt to virtue? I've had to work for the money I've made. But at least I've kept my self-respect.

LEONORA	(*raging*) How dare you? How dare you criticise my life? Do you think it hasn't been slavery to get the little I've got? Do you think it's cost me nothing but a few cheap embraces? How can you, a dried-up old spinster - how can you understand anything of what my life's been? Do you think I haven't had my torments? Do you think I don't envy women who've got respectability, who've got families, who aren't just forgotten or pensioned off when they lose their stock-in-trade?
ELLEN	Then you can't blame me for fighting for my family!
LEONORA	Ellen, you're a frightful hypocrite. You're worse. You're a cheat. You've pretended to be my friend. But it wasn't friendship you felt for me. You meant to batten on me and get the utmost out of me. You wanted to foist your wretched brood on me indefinitely. You wanted to manoeuvre me into a false position and bleed me white. And when I saw through your little scheme you had the insolence to turn on me and abuse me. But you've chosen the wrong woman! (*Going to the kitchen door.*) I suggest you take a month's wages and go.
	(*She stands looking at the seated* ELLEN. *She is shaking with rage. When to her amazement* ELLEN *crumples up. She bursts into tears.*)
ELLEN	Leonora, don't go like that. Don't go, please. I'm absolutely in the wrong. I didn't mean half I said. I'm dreadfully sorry.
LEONORA	(*still quivering*) I should hope you are!
ELLEN	You're quite right about my sisters. They are - peculiar. I don't wonder they've got on your nerves. I think perhaps they've got on mine, too, and that's why I said what I did. But, you

see, I love them. I love them intensely - just
because they are so helpless. They're almost a
religion with me. You're quite right, though,
Leonora. They can't stay here. They must go.
I see that. I'll send them away. I'll arrange it
at once. Only don't send me away too. I've
been so happy here. And I promise everything
shall be the same as before. Only don't send
me away.

(LEONORA, *moved but still hurt, crosses to her
and lays her hand on her arm.*)

LEONORA   Well, I think we'd better both sleep on it,
            Ellen.

            (*She goes quietly and quickly out into the
            kitchen. Almost immediately the door at the
            foot of the stairs opens and* LOUISA *and* EMILY
            *step in. Like wicked children, they have
            obviously been listening. They come softly to
            either side of the sofa where* ELLEN *is still
            sitting. They look rather like three witches as
            they whisper together.*)

LOUISA   Ellen, we've been listening. Isn't she terrible,
            Ellen? She's wicked. Are you going to send
            us away? You promised you wouldn't, you
            know.

ELLEN   (*putting her arms round them*) No, I'm not
            going to send you away.

EMILY   She spoils everything. I wish *she* could go!

LOUISA   But, Ellen, if you're not going to send us
            away, what are you going to do, Ellen?

ELLEN   (*her face is distraught*) I don't know. I shall
            have to think.

LOUISA   Dear Ellen! Always so clever.

            (*Blackout.*)

Scene Three

*Late afternoon, a week later. it has been a fine, hot,
autumnal day, and the light is gathering for a glorious
sunset.*

*The room is empty, but a noise can be heard on the stairway
and almost at once* LEONORA - *still in her blue dress - and*
ELLEN *appear lifting down a large and battered yellow tin
trunk securely corded up.*

LEONORA   My goodness! It is heavy.

ELLEN   Yes. But we've managed it very well.

LEONORA   We couldn't have got it down so easily when
            we first came here. I expect it's moving all
            those bricks and things. It's got our muscles
            up. (*She sits down on the trunk and puts her
            hands to her head.*) My goodness! I feel an
            awful sight.

ELLEN   Your hair's all crooked.

LEONORA   Why not say my wig's slipped and have done
            with it! We're quite alone.

ELLEN   (*arranging* LEONORA'S *wig*) Let me put it straight.

LEONORA   (*purring*) Just like being in a dressing room
            again! It only wants the smell of the grease
            paint and a nice pair of tights! (*Drawing up
            her skirt and eyeing her ankles critically.*)
            Though I don't think my ankles would run to
            them now.

ELLEN   (*who has watched this little by-play
            disapprovingly*) There!

LEONORA   (*rising*) Thanks, dear. Now tell me exactly
            what you want me to do with this.

ELLEN   Let's get it into the scullery first while
            they're still out.

LEONORA   (*as they take up the trunk*) You must have got
           half the foreshore in it!

           (*They carry the trunk out through the kitchen
           door. The convent bell starts. There is a brief
           pause. Then they return.*)

LEONORA   Hullo. There's the Priory bell. It must be six
           o'clock. Bates will be here in a minute.

ELLEN   It isn't Bates.

LEONORA   Oh?

ELLEN   No. I thought we wouldn't have Bates. He's
           so inquisitive. And he talks so. When I went
           into Rochester on Wednesday I arranged for a
           fly at the station to come out. It'll cost a bit
           more, of course, but it's rather less primitive
           than Bates' rickety little trap.

LEONORA   Well, what am I to do about their box?

ELLEN   Let Bates take it to the station tomorrow and
           have it labelled through to London Bridge.
           I'll pick it up there in the evening. It'll be
           quite handy. I've got them a room in the
           Borough.

LEONORA   (*smiling*) I see. You're a regular Machiavelli,
           aren't you?

ELLEN   Well, isn't it much better this way? For them
           to think they're going for a drive round the
           country? And then, before they know where
           they are, I shall have whisked them into the
           train. I think it's kinder this way.

LEONORA   And when am I to expect you back?

ELLEN   I think I'd better stay over the weekend and
           get them settled in. They'll take a lot of
           settling.

LEONORA	Yes, I should. Don't hurry back on my account. I shall be quite all right.
ELLEN	I hate the idea of your being alone here. I almost wish you hadn't let Lucy go on her holiday.
LEONORA	But, my dear, it was your idea that she shouldn't postpone it. I wanted her to wait till they'd gone.
ELLEN	Well, you see, I was afraid that, if she were here when Louisa and Emily went, we mightn't have been able to conceal our little plan from them. And then there'd have been a lot of trouble. Perhaps a scene.
LEONORA	But Lucy needn't have known anything about it.
ELLEN	You never know with the girls. They listen. They overhear things. And they will gossip.
LEONORA	I expect you're right. But we may not be clear of possible scenes yet. Supposing they go up to their rooms and find all their things vanished.
ELLEN	Oh, I'll see they don't.
LEONORA	You were lucky to get Louisa out at all.
ELLEN	Oh, she always does what I want when I insist. There's no reason for them to go upstairs again. I saw to it they were dressed for the journey before I sent them out.
LEONORA	Ellen dear, before they come back, I want to - to give you something. (*She goes to the hearth, unlocks the oven and takes out the cash box.*) I know this is going to put you to a lot of expense. And I expect you'll have a very trying time when they find out the trick you've played on them, and they learn they're not coming back. Now, look here. Here are ten sovereigns. That'll pay for your journey

and a few weeks' rent. And perhaps you'll be
able to buy them one or two little comforts to
make up for their disappointment.

ELLEN   (*taking the money and kissing her, but
                 distantly*) You're much too kind.

LEONORA   I'm so glad we've made everything up. I hate
                 quarrelling. I've got a very hot temper, but it
                 soon evaporates.

ELLEN   I wish I was made like that.

LEONORA   (*kissing her again affectionately*) You're a
                 dear old stick-in-the-mud, Ellen. And I'm
                 very fond of you. I can't think why I thought
                 of parting from you. And I never will! So far
                 as I'm concerned you can stay here for the
                 rest of my life. (*With a change of tone.*) Well,
                 as we're servantless, I'd better go and see
                 about my supper.

ELLEN   There's nothing to be cooked. I've left
                 everything ready.

LEONORA   Yes, but, as I'm all by myself, I think I shall
                 get up a bottle of that champagne Lord
                 Kenardington sent me for Christmas.

ELLEN   (*her lips tightening*) I believe you're going to
                 celebrate my sisters going.

LEONORA   I don't mind telling you, Ellen, I am! This is
                 the first time I shall have been able to call my
                 house my own for months.

ELLEN   (*with an oblique glance*) It'll be the first time
                 you've slept here alone, too, won't it?

LEONORA   I don't suppose even that will worry me with
                 a pint of Clicquot inside me!

ELLEN   I've made a salad. And there's a cold
                 partridge and some cream cheese from the
                 convent.

LEONORA	A bird! Cream cheese! Champagne! It only wants the right setting. A private room at Kettner's - candlelight - distant music. And someone's foot pressing yours - very lightly - under the table. My goodness, Ellen! What am I talking about? Why haven't you stopped me? I'm in a crazy mood today!
	(*She is at the kitchen door.* ELLEN *is by the table on which lies the cash box.*)
ELLEN	(*quietly*) You're leaving your money.
LEONORA	(*darting back*) Oh, mercy! I really am crazy. (*She puts back the cash box in the oven and locks the padlock.*) The bell's been stopped some time. Your sisters ought to be back. (*Coming to* ELLEN.) Ellen, I believe in your heart you're glad to be rid of them, too. Though, of course, you'll never admit it.
	(*The front door opens and* LOUISA *and* EMILY *enter. They look very quaint and un-countrified in their outdoor attire.* EMILY *carries a large spray of autumnal "Traveller's Joy."*)
LOUISA	I hope we're back in time, Ellen, as you told us. Oh, dear! How nice it is to be indoors again!
LEONORA	What have you got there, Miss Emily?
EMILY	Lucy told me it's called "Traveller's Joy."
LEONORA	Hm - very appropriate, when you're going for a drive.
EMILY	It has white flowers in the summer. I remember when we came the hedges were full of it. Do you think, Ellen, it would keep through the winter like sea lavender and honesty?
ELLEN	I don't know, Emily.

LOUISA   Oh, but I expect you do, Ellen. Only you
              won't say. (*Sitting down with a little sigh.*) I
              wish I weren't going for this drive. Do think I
              need to, Ellen?   .

ELLEN   I particularly want you to, darling. I'm giving
              you a great treat.

LOUISA   Yes, dear, I know. But I'd sooner stay in the
              house. It's getting quite evening. And I don't
              like the long shadows.

EMILY   (*letting the "Traveller's Joy" fall to the
              ground*) I'm very glad we're going for a
              drive. And I'm glad it's late. We shall be able
              to see the sun disappear behind the river.

ELLEN   A September evening's the most beautiful
              time of the year. And there's nothing to be
              afraid of. I'm coming with you.

LOUISA   Is Miss Fiske coming, too?

LEONORA   No, You'll be just by yourselves. (*Rather
              naughtily.*) That'll be what you like won't it,
              Miss Louisa?

LOUISA   Yes. Yes.

EMILY   I think I'll go up and get into an easier pair of
              boots. These pinch me rather.

ELLEN   No, you sit down. I'll run up and get them.

LOUISA   No Emily. You mustn't let Ellen wait on you.

ELLEN   It's all right. I've got to go up in any case.
              I've got to get my own bonnet and cloak.

EMILY   They're in the left-hand corner of the
              cupboard.

ELLEN   I'll find them, Emily.

              (*She runs upstairs.*)

LOUISA	Ellen's in one of her bossy moods today, isn't she, Emily?
EMILY	She always orders us about. She won't let us have wills of our own.
LOUISA	I think she's worried about something. I think she's got something on her mind.
LEONORA	Oh, come, Miss Louisa! I don't think that's right. I've noticed nothing different about her.
LOUISA	But then you wouldn't, would you? You're not one of the family. I know Ellen's worried about something. I can tell it.
EMILY	(*beginning to take off her boots*) I wonder if we are just going for a drive. I wonder if she's sending us away.
LOUISA	(*in immediate agitation*) Don't say that Emily! Oh, I do hope it's not true. But you'd know, Miss Fiske, wouldn't you? You're not both sending us away, are you?
LEONORA	(*artfully*) Do you think I should know - not being one of the family?
LOUISA	No, no. I suppose that's true. I suppose you wouldn't. Ellen would arrange that by herself, wouldn't she?
EMILY	If Ellen tries to send me away, I shan't go.
LOUISA	Oh, but we must do what Ellen tells us, mustn't we? I don't know what would become of us if we offended Ellen.
EMILY	She might take me to the station, but I wouldn't get into the train.
LEONORA	I think you're both imagining much too much.

LOUISA	Yes. I think we are. I think you're right. I don't think Ellen would deceive us.
EMILY	(*suddenly, looking towards the window*) What's become of your telescope, Louisa?
LOUISA	It's on the window sill, dear.
EMILY	No, it isn't.
LOUISA	(*rising agitatedly*) Isn't it? Where is it? It was here when I went out! I knew I oughtn't to have gone out! I knew something would happen.
LEONORA	It's quite all right, Miss Louisa. Ellen took it out into the kitchen. I think she was going to clean it.
LOUISA	Oh, no, she wasn't. I always do that myself. Why has she taken it into the kitchen? I believe it's been broken! I must get it! I must have it!
LEONORA	I promise you it's not been broken. If you'll wait here, I'll get it for you.
LOUISA	No, I wish to get it.
LEONORA	(*snapping*) I'm sorry, but you can't.
EMILY	(*sullenly*) Why shouldn't Louisa get it herself?
LEONORA	(*going to the kitchen door*) Because it happens to be my kitchen and Miss Louisa's my guest.
LOUISA	(*following her*) I'm going to get it! (*She feebly seizes* LEONORA *and there is an undignified little struggle at the door, which ends by* LEONORA *forcing* LOUISA *on to the piano stool.*)
LEONORA	Please sit down, Miss Louisa. Don't you realise you're making the most ridiculous scene about absolutely nothing?

(*She goes quickly out into the kitchen.* LOUISA *sobs.*)

LOUISA It's broken! I know it's broken!

EMILY I don't think Ellen broke it. I think she broke it. She wasn't really angry when she spoke like that. She was only saying it to cover up something.

LOUISA Oh, how I hate her!

EMILY Ellen wouldn't like you to say that. They're together again - she and Ellen. I think they're in league together.

LOUISA I wish you wouldn't keep saying things against Ellen, Emily!

EMILY You think Ellen's perfect, don't you? You'll find out about her one day.

(ELLEN *comes down the stairs. She is wearing her bonnet and cloak, and carries a pair of ladies' elastic-sided boots.*)

ELLEN (*giving* EMILY *the boots*) Here are your boots, Emily.

EMILY Thank you, Ellen.

ELLEN What's the matter, Louisa darling?

LOUISA (*tearfully*) Ellen! Someone's broken my telescope.

ELLEN Have they, dear? Oh, no. I don't think they can have.

LOUISA But why did you take it out into the kitchen?

ELLEN I didn't.

LOUISA (*excitedly*) There, Emily! She was lying. She was lying.

ELLEN	Who was? Who was lying?
LOUISA	Miss Fiske! She said you'd taken it into the kitchen to clean it. She's gone to fetch it now. I knew you wouldn't have.
ELLEN	(*suddenly, remembering that, of course, the telescope is packed*) Oh! Oh yes, of course. It's all right, darling. I'd forgotten. I did take it out. It's quite true.
LOUISA	You're only humouring me because you know it's broken.
ELLEN	(*sharply*) Nonsense, Louisa. Stop being silly.
EMILY	(*suddenly*) These are not my boots, Ellen. They're yours.
ELLEN	Yes, I know, dear. I'm making you a present of them. You always do have my old ones, don t you?
EMILY	Thank you. But I wish you'd brought me my own. My feet ache, and yours always take a little getting accustomed to.
ELLEN	Well, you won't have to do any walking on your drive.
	(LEONORA *enters, from the kitchen in triumph, with the telescope.* EMILY *begins grudgingly to put on the boots* ELLEN *has brought.*)
LEONORA	Here we are! You see, Miss Louisa? It's not broken. It's as right as ninepence.
LOUISA	(*seizing it*) Oh, thank you. I am glad to have it. No, it hasn't been broken. But it hasn't been cleaned.
ELLEN	I haven't had time yet.
LEONORA	(*laughing*) Miss Louisa was so agitated I believe she thought I was going to steal it, Ellen.

ELLEN	(*to* LOUISA, *tenderly*) It was just a lot of fuss about nothing, wasn't it?
LOUISA	Yes, dear! I was very silly. But it's not nothing to me.
LEONORA	(*going to the stairs*) Ellen, call me when the fly comes. I'd like to see you all safely off.
EMILY	(*resentfully*) There's no need for you to trouble. We shall be back in two hours, shan't we?
LEONORA	(*with almost a wink at* ELLEN) Well, I'd like to make sure you start comfortably.
	(*She hurries upstairs.*)
LOUISA	Emily says that we're not really going for a drive. That you're sending us away. That we're not coming back. That's not true, is it, Ellen?
ELLEN	Of course it's not true. What made you think that, Emily?
EMILY	You see, Miss Fiske doesn't like us. And she's been so different, so friendly. Almost as if she knew she were getting rid of us.
ELLEN	Well, you're both wrong. You're coming back. I promise you that. And I've always kept my promises to you, haven't I?
LOUISA	Yes, Ellen. You have - always.
EMILY	She seemed very anxious to come and say goodbye to us.
ELLEN	We may be saying goodbye to her.
EMILY	What do you mean, Ellen?
ELLEN	I want you to keep a little secret. Will you promise me?

Louisa	Yes, Ellen. Of course we promise.
Ellen	And you, too, Emily. You must promise, too.
Emily	Very well, I promise you, Ellen.
Ellen	(*she goes to the stairway door and closes it*) You're very happy here, aren't you? You like this place?
Louisa	Yes, Ellen.
Emily	Yes, Ellen. We're very happy.
Ellen	You'd be happier still, wouldn't you, if we were here by ourselves?
Louisa	Oh, yes, Ellen. She spoils everything.
Emily	But it's her house. How could we be here by ourselves?
Ellen	That's what I want to tell you. I'm going to try and persuade her to sell it to me.
Louisa	Oh, how clever, Ellen! Then she could go away and live somewhere else.
Emily	But supposing she wants too much money for it. Ellen? She may want more than you're prepared to pay.
Ellen	I'm prepared to pay quite a big price, really.
Emily	I didn't think you had all that much money, Ellen.
Ellen	Oh, I've saved quite a lot.
Louisa	(*trembling with excitement*) Oh it will be lovely if it can be ours! I'm so excited, Ellen. When will you know? When will you ask her?
Ellen	I'm going to ask her today. That's one of the reasons for the drive. I want to get you out of the place. I want to tackle her by myself.

EMILY   But you're coming out with us.

ELLEN   Only as far as the Priory. Then I shall get out and slip back. And you'll go for your drive around.

LOUISA   Oh, I shall tell the man to hurry! We mustn't be away too long. I shall be so anxious to know.

ELLEN   That's just what I don't want. I want you to give me at least two hours. It's a complicated thing to arrange, you know. It can't be done in five minutes. I want to get it all fixed up before you come back.

EMILY   But why should you come with us at all, Ellen?

(ELLEN *does not answer.*)

Ellen, why should you come with us at all?

ELLEN   I want to call at the convent.

LOUISA   But why must you call there, Ellen? Father wouldn't have liked your calling at the convent.

ELLEN   (*after a moment*) I want to get the Reverend Mother on our side. She has great influence with Miss Fiske. I want her to help me to persuade her.

LOUISA   Oh, of course. Oh, how clever you are, Ellen! I should never have thought of that.

(ELLEN *goes to the half-moon table and takes a devotional book from it.*)

ELLEN   Now, look here, Louisa. Here's a Bible. I want you to put your hand on it and swear on Father's memory that you'll never repeat what I've told you about buying the house as long as you live.

LOUISA	Yes, Ellen. If you wish, Ellen. But it rather frightens me. What do I say?
ELLEN	Just say, "I promise."
LOUISA	I promise.
ELLEN	You, too, Emily.
EMILY	I won't swear on the Bible. It's wicked.
LOUISA	Oh, Emily! You must do what Ellen says.
ELLEN	If you won't promise me, Emily, I shan't buy the house. And I shall send you both back to London.
LOUISA	Oh, Ellen - not that, please. Emily, do be sensible.
EMILY	Very well. But I don't like being made to do things. I promise.
	(*There comes a sudden rat-tat-tat at the front door.*)
LOUISA	Oh, dear! What's that?
ELLEN	(*looking through the open window*) It's the man from Rochester with the carriage. (*Calling.*) All right! We'll be out in a minute!
MAN'S VOICE	(*off*) Very good, Mum. I'll turn the 'orses. Which way d'ye want to go?
ELLEN	We'll tell you later. (*Leaving the window.*) Now, come along, my darlings.
LOUISA	(*like an excited child*) Oh, wouldn't it be lovely if when we came back, we found that you'd bought the house and she'd gone!
ELLEN	(*turning on her almost savagely*) Will you be quiet!

LOUISA	Oh, don't! Don't be cross with me, Ellen!
ELLEN	You've just sworn on the Bible never to mention it again!
LOUISA	(*awed*) I'm sorry. I thought it didn't count when we were together.
ELLEN	She might have overheard you and that would have spoilt everything. It's better for us not to discuss it even among ourselves.
LOUISA	(*meekly*) Whatever you say, Ellen.

(LEONORA *enters from the stairway door.*)

LEONORA	Did I hear the carriage?
ELLEN	Yes. It's just come. We're going now.
LEONORA	I do hope you all have a nice drive.
LOUISA	I expect we shall come back very hungry.
ELLEN	Now, come along.

(*As they go out of the front door.*)

LOUISA	Oh, it is a high step, isn't it, from the ground? You'll have to help me, Ellen.
ELLEN	The driver will lift you up.
LOUISA	Oh, that will be fun! Won't it, Emily?

(*They disappear.* LEONORA *watches their departure.*)

LEONORA	Goodbye. Make the most of it! Have you told the driver which way, Ellen?
ELLEN	(*calling back*) He knows.
LEONORA	(*waving*) Au revoir!

(*The sound of the carriage is heard rumbling away.* LEONORA *closes the front door, with*

*obvious relief. The room is now full of
evening sunlight.)*

Oh, thank God for that!

(She picks up EMILY'S *pair of boots with a
little grimace and then the fallen strands of
creeper, exclaiming grimly as she does so.
"Traveller's Joy." She then collects* LOUISA'S
*telescope and with a little laugh, shoulders it
like a rifle. She marches out through the
kitchen door singing.)*

"For he's going to marry Yum-Yum—Yum-
Yum!"

*(The sound of the singing continues outside.
Then* ELLEN *enters swiftly and silently by the
front door. She hurries across the room to the
stairway which she mounts quickly but
furtively. The grandfather clock strikes six,
then* LEONORA *returns, still singing gaily to
herself. She carries an open bottle of
champagne and a glass and a couple of turves
of peat. She puts the champagne and glass on
the piano and then crosses and lays the peat
on the fire. She returns to the piano and,
pouring out a glass of wine, toasts herself in
silent compliance. She is evidently preparing
for an evening. Then she sits at the piano and
opens the "Mikado" score. She begins to play
"Tit-Willow". When she is halfway through
the verse the stairway door opens very slowly
and quietly.* ELLEN *is standing there, her face
taut and tense. She has discarded her bonnet
and cloak, and in her hands is the cord of a
pink silk dressing gown. She advances a step
or two, but* LEONORA *does not hear and goes
on with her playing. Blackout.)*

Typical Nun - calm
No nerves, no hotching
But nosey!
Don't talk to her much, look around

ACT TWO

Scene One

A wild night in mid-November. There is a violent storm of rain and wind in progress.

The room is empty. It is cosily lighted by one or two oil lamps, and a great log fire roars in the hearth. The two little candles in front of the figure of the Virgin are alight. The curtains are drawn. Everything is bright and shining in the warm glow, and the whole feeling is one of snugness.

As the lights rise there comes a rapid knocking at the front door. LUCY *enters from the kitchen, crosses the room and opens the door.* SISTER THERESA *enters, a fat, red-faced, jolly old nun with gleaming gold spectacles. She carries a huge, dripping umbrella and a storm lantern.*

THERESA   Is Miss Creed at home?

LUCY   Yes, Sister. They're all three at home. Which one do you want?

THERESA   Oh, Miss Ellen, please. I wonder if I could sit here for a minute. Unless, of course, Miss Fiske has returned.

LUCY   No. She's still away. Let me take your umbrella into the scullery. (*She relieves her of it.*) I'll stand it in the sink.

THERESA   (*setting her lantern on the floor*) Yes. It is coming down. Cats and dogs. And so sudden, too. After such a beautiful afternoon.

LUCY   You sit down by the fire, Sister. I'll tell Miss Creed. She's in the kitchen.

THERESA   (*going to the hearth*) You *have* got a roaring fire.

             (LUCY *goes, just as* LOUISA *enters from the stairway.*)

LOUISA   (*startled at seeing the nun sitting there*) Oh!

THERESA	Good evening.
LOUISA	Are you waiting to see my sister?
THERESA	Yes.
LOUISA	Oh.
THERESA	I understand Miss Fiske's still away.
LOUISA	Oh, yes. She's not here.
THERESA	For the moment I thought she was back - when I saw the candles.
LOUISA	(*turning a little shrinkingly to the altar*) Oh, the candles? Yes. Ellen's taken to lighting them. I don't quite know why. I'm sure Father wouldn't have approved. But she likes to do it because she thinks Miss Fiske would have liked her to. She says it keeps her memory burning.
THERESA	What a very kind thought of your sister's!
LOUISA	Ellen's full of kind thoughts. She's so clever.
	(ELLEN *enters from the kitchen.*)
ELLEN	I'm sorry to have kept you waiting, Sister. But we're in the middle of making our quince jam.
THERESA	Please - you mustn't apologise. I've been chatting very happily to your sister.
ELLEN	(*with a slight reaction*) Oh? I hope she's not been tiresome. We were brought up as very strict Non-conformists, you know. And my sisters are rather apt sometimes to - well, to voice their prejudices, I'm afraid.
LOUISA	But I said nothing, Ellen! Nothing at all!
THERESA	(*blandly*) Whatever our religions are, we can always be good neighbours, can't we?

ELLEN   (*smiling*) Of course.

THERESA   And I'm here with a neighbourly request, I'm
                 afraid. We're rather in trouble at the Priory.
                 Our supply of oil hasn't arrived from
                 Rochester. They forgot it yesterday, and I
                 suppose the storm has prevented them coming
                 today. We've absolutely run out. I wondered
                 if I might borrow a can over the weekend -
                 that is, if you can spare it. We'll pay you
                 back as soon as our supply arrives. It's sure to
                 be here on Monday.

ELLEN   Of course I will. Louisa, go into the scullery
                 and bring me one of those gallon cans of
                 paraffin.

LOUISA   Oh, please, Ellen, couldn't Lucy do it?

ELLEN   No, darling. Lucy's busy with the jam. Run
                 along. Do what you're told.

                 (LOUISA *goes.* ELLEN *and the nun are sitting on
                 the two settles.*)

THERESA   It's very peaceful here sitting in this lovely
                 old chimney corner. People miss such a lot in
                 towns.

ELLEN   Oh, yes. We're pre-Tudor. The Priory's very
                 old, too, isn't it?

THERESA   Yes. It was a monastery at one time. It goes
                 back to Henry the Fourth. I wish you could
                 come and see us some day.

ELLEN   Thank you.

THERESA   Is this one of the old bake-ovens?

ELLEN   Yes. We don't use it now, though.

THERESA   No. All the old customs are dying out. Such a
                 pity. I think it's a very nice thought of yours
                 to keep Miss Fiske's candles alight while
                 she's away.

ELLEN	(*alertly*) Oh, did Louisa tell you about that?
THERESA	I'm afraid I asked her. I thought, when I saw them, Miss Fiske might be home.
ELLEN	Oh, no.
THERESA	When are you expecting her back? We miss her so much at the convent.
ELLEN	I don't know. I haven't heard from her quite recently.
THERESA	Is she in London?
ELLEN	She went to London to begin with. Then she was going on - elsewhere.
THERESA	The Reverend Mother was wondering what she ought to do about the rent for that little three acre field we hire from her. It's only a few pounds, but we like to pay our debts promptly.
ELLEN	Well, I'm managing all her affairs while she's away, so if you send it to me I'll be responsible for it and forward it when I get her next address. Of course, I'll let you have a receipt for it.
THERESA	Thank you. That sounds a very good arrangement. I'll tell the Reverend Mother.

(LOUISA *enters from the kitchen with a large can of oil.*)

LOUISA	I've got it, Ellen, but it's rather heavy.
THERESA	Oh, thank you so much.
ELLEN	You'll want some help, won't you?
THERESA	Oh, no. I can manage.
ELLEN	You can't carry this and your lantern and your umbrella, can you? I'll get Lucy to go down with you.

THERESA   But what about your jam? It wouldn't be very
               neighbourly of me if I let you spoil that.

ELLEN   (*at the kitchen door*) Lucy! I want you to go
               down to the Priory with the Sister. And bring
               her umbrella. You'll have to wrap up. It's still
               pouring. I'll watch the jam. (*Turning to* SISTER
               THERESA.) Well, you'll excuse me if I say
               good night, won't you?

THERESA   Of course. And you have been kind. Thank
               you so much.

               (ELLEN *goes into the kitchen.*)

LOUISA   I think you're so brave going out in the dark
               and the wet. I hate the dark. I'm always glad
               when morning comes.

THERESA   (*smiling*) I never worry about things like that.
               I believe we're watched over.

LOUISA   I think that, too. But I'm never quite sure
               who's watching us.

               (EMILY *enters from the stairway. She carries a
               tray with a little wooden box, a pot of warm
               glue and a pile of sea shells. She starts when
               she sees* THERESA, *just as* LOUISA *did.*)

EMILY   I didn't know anyone was here.

LOUISA   It's all right, Emily. Ellen knows. And she's
               just going (*To* THERESA.) It's my sister Emily.

THERESA   Good evening.

EMILY   It isn't a very good one, is it?

               (*She puts her tray on the table and sets to
               work at once, sticking the shells in patterns
               on the wooden box.*)

THERESA   Well, it is wild. But then we must expect this
               in November.

EMILY	I was down by the river wall today, and a lot of ships went out to sea.
LOUISA	In this wind? Oh, the poor sailors!
THERESA	At any rate, I hope our friend isn't on the sea tonight.
EMILY	What do you mean - our friend?
THERESA	I meant Miss Fiske.
EMILY	We don't mind where she is.

(LUCY *enters from the kitchen. She is wearing a hooded cloak and galoshes and carries two umbrellas, the Sister's and her own.*)

LUCY	I'm quite ready, Sister.
THERESA	Well, good night.
LOUISA	Good night.
THERESA	Good night, Miss Emily.

(*There is a pause.* EMILY *does not reply.*)

	What very pretty work you're doing!
LOUISA	Oh, Emily's very clever with her fingers.
THERESA	It's very nicely done indeed. May I look? Oh, very nice. Do you sell them?
EMILY	(*in wonderment*) Could I sell it?
LUCY	Why, yes, Miss. I'm sure you could. They're very fashionable. I saw lots of shell boxes like that when I was on my holidays at Hastings.
EMILY	I never thought of doing that. I only make them because it uses up the shells.
THERESA	(*to* LUCY) Well, now, my dear, if you're coming I think we should go. Thank you again. Good bye.

LOUISA	Good bye.

(THERESA *takes up the lantern and the can, and she and* LUCY *go out of the front door,* LUCY *opening the great umbrella as they go.* LOUISA *shuts and bolts the door after them. Then she comes and sits on the settle.*)

I think that nun is rather a nice old woman. She'd look like a farmer's wife if she didn't wear that horrid dress. I wonder if we're wrong in not making friends with the nuns.

EMILY	I hate them. You know what Father always said about Romans.
LOUISA	Ellen was very nice to her. They were quite chatty together.
EMILY	You never can tell what Ellen's thinking. Louisa, I think Ellen's changing. I hope she's not going to get in league with the nuns against us.
LOUISA	Ellen would never do that, Emily.
EMILY	She's taken to lighting those candles.
LOUISA	Yes, I don't think that's right, do you?
EMILY	(*suddenly, rising*) I think I'll blow them out.
LOUISA	You mustn't do that, Emily! Ellen wouldn't like that.
EMILY	Why should Ellen have everything her own way?

(*She walks boldly to the altar and blows out the candles.*)

LOUISA	(*half admiringly, half terrified*) Oh, Emily! What have you done?
EMILY	(*returning to the table*) Something I wanted to do.

(*There is suddenly a violent knocking at the front door.*)

LOUISA   That must be Lucy. She's back soon.

(*She unbolts and opens it. To her amazement* ALBERT FEATHER *bursts in. He is wearing an ulster and a deerstalker's cap. He is absolutely drenched. He carries a little dark lantern with which he has been picking his way along. He makes a mock-dramatic entrance.* LOUISA, *not recognising him, recoils with a shrill scream.*)

ALBERT   Why, if it isn't Aunt Emily. Or is it Aunt Louisa? All right. Don't look so scared. I shan't eat you.

LOUISA   (*aghast*) Who are you?

ALBERT   I'm Albert. Albert Feather.

EMILY   (*rising*) It's Albert, Louisa. Rose's boy.

LOUISA   Oh! Albert? Rose's boy? Yes. So it is.

(ALBERT *shuts the door, but does not bolt it.*)

LOUISA   Of course. Come in, Albert. Oh, you are wet! You're wet through. We must tell Ellen. Will you tell her, Emily, or shall I?

EMILY   You tell her.

(ELLEN *appears in the kitchen doorway. She is keyed-up and tense.*)

ELLEN   I heard a man's voice. Who is it?

LOUISA   It's our nephew, Ellen. It's Albert. And we haven't seen him for years!

ELLEN   What? Albert? What on earth are you doing here?

ALBERT   I've walked over from Gravesend.

ELLEN   (*kissing him*) What! Tonight?

ALBERT   It was fine when I started.

ELLEN   Well, sit down by the fire and take your boots off. And your ulster. My goodness, you are wet! You must be soaked through.

ALBERT   I'll soon get dry. This fire'll do the trick.

                 (*They get him to the fire, cosseting him. They take off his overcoat and coat.* EMILY *takes his little lantern from him.*)

ELLEN   (*giving his clothes to* EMILY) Here, take these into the kitchen, Emily. And hang them on the clothes horse in front of the stove. Don't put them too near the grate. And stay by the jam and see that it doesn't burn till Lucy gets back.

EMILY   (*surly*) Oh, very well.

                 (*She goes, rebellious at being ordered.*)

ALBERT   It's awfully good of you, Aunt Ellen, but what I really want most is a bit of grub and something nice and warm to chase it down the hatchway. I haven't had anything since breakfast.

ELLEN   Of course. I'll get you something. And, Louisa, run up to the front room and bring down that dressing gown. It's only a woman's, Albert, but it'll be better than nothing.

LOUISA   Oh, yes. You - you mean the pink one? Will it matter?

ELLEN   Why should it?

LOUISA   Supposing she sends for it one day.

                 (*She goes upstairs without waiting for a reply.*)

ALBERT	I say! It is a change for a bachelor. To be waited on by three lovely ladies.
ELLEN	You silly billy, why didn't you write and tell me you were coming?
ALBERT	I'll tell you all about that when I'm dry outside and not so dry in.

(ELLEN *goes out into the kitchen, laughing.* ALBERT *looks round the room, at the dresser and at* EMILY'S *shells. Then* LUCY *enters from the front door. At first she does not see him. She turns and bolts the door.*)

(*suddenly*) What cheer, Lucy!

LUCY	(*jumping*) Oh! You did give me a start.
ALBERT	(*airily*) Just a little habit of mine.
LUCY	(*recognising him*) Why, it's you! So you've turned up again?
ALBERT	Yes. Bad pennies do, you know. Pleased to see me?
LUCY	I'm surprised.
ALBERT	(*jauntily*) The other'll come later. Still a shortage of male fish in the estuary, duckie?
LUCY	There's a new shepherd over at Cooling, but no one's seen him yet.
ALBERT	And he's probably eighty and a bit. (*Rather anxiously.*) Here, Lucy. Tell us. Is Miss Fiske about?
LUCY	No. She's away.
ALBERT	(*relieved*) That's a bit of luck. Listen, Lucy. Does my Aunt Ellen know I blew over last summer?

LUCY	Not that I know of. I've never heard talk of it. I've said nothing. Miss Fiske told me not to.
ALBERT	Good. Then I may be all right.
LUCY	What have you come over for this time?
ALBERT	Need you ask? To get a glimpse of your bonny, bright eyes, of course!
LUCY	I see you haven't changed. You're just as fast.
ALBERT	(*there is a noise on the stairs*) Shut up! Here's one of the old gals. We don't know each other, remember. (*Slyly.*) Not that we shan't later.
LUCY	I'm very particular who I know.

(*She goes off into the kitchen, her head in the air.* LOUISA *comes down the stairs with a wonderful pink silk dressing gown. This, having belonged to* LEONORA, *is slightly outre and Parisian.*)

LOUISA	I've got it down for you, Albert. Oh, was that Lucy?
ALBERT	(*innocently*) I don't know, Auntie. It was the servant. Is her name Lucy?
LOUISA	No. Of course you wouldn't know, dear, would you? Now, see if this fits.

(*He puts it on. The effect is grotesque.*)

ALBERT	Woa, my hearties! The hansom cabbie's delight! (*He throws himself into an exaggeratedly feminine attitude.*) I say, Aunt Louisa! Shouldn't I be a riot on the halls? Ta-ra-ra-boom-de-ay! Ta-ra-ra-boom-de-ay!

(LOUISA *shouts with laughter. He takes a few dance steps and she imitates him.* EMILY *enters from the kitchen.* ALBERT *rushes to her and dances her round the room.*)

ALBERT   Ta-ra-ra-boom-de-ay!

EMILY   (*shrilly as she struggles*) Don't do it, Albert!

ALBERT   There you are, me old cup of tea.

       (*He picks her up and plants her in a sitting position on the tray of shells on the table.*)

EMILY   Don't do it, Albert. It's all glue!

LOUISA   (*going into fits of laughter*) Oh, the shells are sticking to her skirt! Isn't he funny!

       (ELLEN *has entered from the kitchen. She carries a tray on which are a plate of cold beef, some bread, grapes and an apple, and a bottle of cognac.*)

ELLEN   Now, Albert, behave. Louisa, put Emily's tray on the piano.

       (LOUISA *obeys.* ELLEN *puts* ALBERT'S *tray on the table in place of* EMILY'S.)

       Here's your food.

ALBERT   My word, Aunt Ellen! What a spread! Cold cow and a bottle of the best. (*He picks up the bottle with interest.*) Cognac, 1830. Where did you pinch this, Auntie?

ELLEN   Now, pull yourself together, Louisa. Stop laughing and get him a glass. No, bring two. I think I'll have a little to keep him company.

       (LOUISA *goes to the dresser and brings the glasses.*)

ALBERT   And bring a couple of those egg cups. You and Aunt Emily must whet your whistle, too.

LOUISA   Whet our whistle? Oh, Albert, you *are* silly. Do you think we might, Ellen? I've never tasted cognac.

EMILY   (*fetching the egg cups*) Of course we can,
                 Louisa. He asked us.

ELLEN   I don't think you'd better.

ALBERT   (*dispensing the drinks*) Oh, come on, Auntie!
                 You don't have a nephew here every night of
                 the week! Here's your ration of grog, Aunt
                 Ellen. And a thimbleful for the Belle of the
                 Ball, Miss Emily Creed!

EMILY   Not so much, Albert, please.

ALBERT   (*as* LOUISA *presents her egg cup*) And what
                 have we here? That wrecker of homes, Miss
                 Louisa. Here's a nice drop of liquid to water
                 your garden, me old stick of celery.

LOUISA   Oh, Ellen, isn't he funny? I shall die.

ALBERT   Now then, gals, down the hatchway! Wait a
                 minute. (*Suavely.*) I'll give you a toast. Our
                 Beloved Queen. (*They all rise loyally. Then
                 he suddenly grimaces.*) The Queen of the
                 Cannibal Isle!

ELLEN   Now, Albert, settle down and eat your supper.
                 You'll upset your aunts, you know.

LOUISA   Oh, do let him go on, Ellen. He's just like a play.

EMILY   You've never been to a play.

LOUISA   No, I know. But I'm sure he's just like one.
                 Have you ever been to a play, Albert?

ALBERT   (*in shocked tones*) Oh, no, Aunt Louisa.
                 Never. Theatres are haunts of vice. I should
                 never lower myself.

LOUISA   (*crushed*) Oh, I'm sorry, Albert. I always say
                 the wrong thing, don't I?

ALBERT   Don't apologise. (*Refilling their glasses.*)
                 Now then, gals, drink up. One more, Aunt
                 Ellen.

ELLEN   No, Albert, no.

ALBERT   And a nip for the Siamese twins. Now, my
                 lords, ladies and gentlemen, I give you
                 another toast. The toast of absent friends.
                 And, so far as I'm concerned the longer
                 they're absent the better.

EMILY   Absent friends.

                 (*All but* ELLEN *raise their glasses and drink.*)

LOUISA   Absent friends. I suppose we ought to think
                 about Miss Fiske, Ellen. But she was never
                 exactly a friend, was she?

ELLEN   Now we've had quite enough of this nonsense.
                 I'm going to put the bottle away. You get on
                 with your supper, Albert. And you be off to
                 bed, Emily and Louisa.

EMILY   (*sullenly*) I don't want to go to bed.

LOUISA   Oh, let us stop up and talk to Albert, Ellen.

ELLEN   No, my darlings. You've had quite enough
                 excitement. You'll be able to talk to Albert in
                 the morning. I want to talk to him now.

ALBERT   Go on. Be good little girls. Toddle off to bye-
                 bye.

LOUISA   Very well. I suppose we must.

EMILY   Good night, Albert.

LOUISA   Fancy! Rose's boy - at our table. After all
                 these years - all our family under one roof.
                 And Ellen's roof, too! It's too good to be true,
                 Emily.

                 (ELLEN *is staring at the extinguished candles.*)

ELLEN   (*in a strange voice*) Who put out those
                 candles?

LOUISA   What candles, Ellen? Oh, those!

EMILY   It must have been the wind.

           (*And she goes upstairs.*)

LOUISA   Good night, Albert.

ALBERT   Good night, Empress.

LOUISA   (*at the foot of the stairs, looking back slyly*) It
           - it wasn't the wind, Ellen.

           (*She follows* EMILY. ELLEN *relights the candles
           with a taper lit at the fire.* ALBERT *proceeds to
           attack his meal.*)

ALBERT   They're like a couple of old children, aren't
           they? I say, Aunt Ellen, you've not turned
           Papist, have you?

ELLEN   No, Albert.

ALBERT   I was wondering. They'd be playing musical
           chairs in the family vault if you did.

ELLEN   (*the candles are now relighted*) I do this for a
           friend. I suppose you want to stay the night?

ALBERT   Well, I do rather. Actually I was wondering if
           you could put me up for a little longer.

ELLEN   Well, you'll have to shake down on the sofa
           in here for tonight. I've told Lucy to bring
           you in the carriage rug when she's finished
           bottling the jam.

ALBERT   I don't mind where I doss.

ELLEN   Tomorrow we can get the front room ready
           for you. Why have you been so long in
           coming to see me, Albert?

ALBERT   I never have any time, Auntie.

ELLEN   Then how do you come to have it now?

ALBERT   Well, it's a compulsory holiday, as you might say.

ELLEN   (*startled*) What? Have you lost your situation
          at the bank?

ALBERT   I've given it up.

ELLEN   Given it up? Oh, you foolish boy! It had such
          good prospects.

ALBERT   Yes, Auntie. That was my trouble. It was all
          prospects and, er, no foreground. Not enough
          ready, you know.

ELLEN   But you couldn't expect to start at the top.
          Besides - think! A bank's so safe. You're so
          secure. You'd have been there for life.

ALBERT   I'm too much of a rolling stone. That's what
          it is.

ELLEN   Ah, like your father - horrid common little
          man. Have you got another job to go to?

ALBERT   'Fraid I haven't.

ELLEN   Well, you'll have to busy yourself to find one.
          It's no good your staying on here. There's
          nothing here. We're out in the wilds.

ALBERT   I know. (*Looking at her shrewdly.*) That's
          why I've come.

ELLEN   (*interpreting his glance*) Albert, you haven't
          done anything - wrong, have you?

ALBERT   Not exactly wrong, Auntie. I just helped
          myself to a little salary I wasn't entitled to.

ELLEN   (*with an intake of her breath*) Do you mean
          you've taken money?

ALBERT   Well, you see - a friend of mine's made a
          hobby of studying keys. And I'm afraid I took
          a few lessons from him.

ELLEN   Have you stolen from the bank?

ALBERT   This is rattling good brandy, Auntie.

ELLEN   Albert, answer me!

ALBERT   You've got it, Auntie.

ELLEN   But if you were so desperately in need of
             money, why didn't you come to your family?

ALBERT   I've got no family but you and the old canary
             bird. And I thought you were on the rocks.

ELLEN   (*a little taken aback*) I did lose my money.
             But I've got some of it back since. I could
             always have found you a few pounds.

ALBERT   A few pounds wouldn't have seen me through it.

ELLEN   (*horrified*) Is it as bad as that? How could
             you, Albert?

ALBERT   (*almost but not quite ashamed*) I know. I know.

ELLEN   I suppose you got into low company. Now tell
             me the worst. What's happened? Can the
             money be put back, or have they found out?

ALBERT   They've found out. They've set the police on me.

ELLEN   (*now thoroughly alarmed*) The police?

ALBERT   Yes. I was having breakfast in the back
             basement this morning when I was given the
             tip they were coming up the steps to the front
             door. So I slipped out into the yard, nipped
             over the wall and down the alley.

ELLEN   But they'll follow you! They'll come here!

ALBERT   Not they. I knew the back way out of
             Gravesend. And it was easy enough once I got
             to the marshes. They might be the edge of the
             world. I haven't met a soul.

ELLEN	(*slightly reassured*) But they're bound to search!
ALBERT	Not here. No one knows I've got relations here. I'm safe here for a lifetime.
ELLEN	Well. you're certainly not going to stay here for a lifetime!
ALBERT	No, of course not. But you'll let me stay here for a week or two, won't you? Till it all blows over. They're not going to waste a lot of the ratepayer's money looking for a hundred pounds they haven't a hope of getting back.
ELLEN	A hundred pounds? What have you done with it? Have you still got it?
ALBERT	No. That burnt a hole long ago. One and ninepence is the state of my current account.
ELLEN	But what do you propose to do?
ALBERT	(*discarding the dressing gown which he throws on the piano stool*) I want to get out of the country and start afresh. Anywhere. America - Australia - I don't care where. I wondered if you'd let me hide here till it's safe, and then advance me my passage money. It wouldn't cost much - steerage.
ELLEN	I suppose that's the only thing I can do.
	(LUCY *enters from the kitchen with a rug.*)
LUCY	I've bottled the jam, Miss. And here's the rug for the gentleman.
ELLEN	Thank you, Lucy. And now you'd better be off to bed.
LUCY	Right, Miss. Will it be one more for breakfast in the morning?
ELLEN	Yes.

ALBERT	Better make it two, if not three. I get an appetite like a whale in the mornings.
LUCY	Good night, Miss.
ELLEN	Good night, Lucy.
LUCY	Good night, Sir.
ALBERT	(*artfully*) Good night - Lucy, is it?
LUCY	(*giving him a look*) Yes. Lucy.

(*She goes out through the kitchen.* ELLEN *arranges the rug on the sofa.*)

ALBERT	I shall sleep better tonight than I've slept for weeks. There's no need for you to wait on me like that, Auntie. I'll tuck myself up.
ELLEN	Very well, Albert. I think I'll go up to bed, too. You'll put the lamp out, won't you?
ALBERT	(*taking a cigar from his vest pocket*) I think I'll just have a weed first. The solitary survivor of the wreck.
ELLEN	(*as he lights it*) Oh, Albert, I hope you're not taking this too lightly. You sound so horribly callous. You have told me the worst, haven't you? There isn't anything else?
ALBERT	What else?
ELLEN	(*she has* LOUISA'S *dressing gown in her hand, and her voice sounds very odd as she says it*) Well, there are worse things than stealing.
ALBERT	Do you mean - have I put someone to sleep? (*He laughs.*) Good Lord, no. I'm not that bad. What a funny old stick you are, Auntie - thinking of such a thing even! I may be a little light-fingered, but there's no blood on my hands. Besides, I'd be too scared. Putting people out calls for real nerve, you know.

ELLEN   (*taking up one of the lamps*) Yes.

                     (*She goes to the foot of the stairway carrying
                     the lamp and the dressing gown.*)

ALBERT   I'm sorry to be such a bird of ill-omen.

ELLEN   Never mind. I dare say it's Providence. Good
                     night, Albert.

ALBERT   Good night, Aunt Ellen.

                     (*She goes upstairs.* ALBERT *draws from his
                     trouser pocket a little bunch of skeleton keys.
                     Rather furtively he deftly shuts the door at the
                     foot of the stairs and turns the key in the lock.
                     Then he opens the kitchen door and listens.
                     All is quiet. He goes to the hearth and
                     examines the padlock on the bake-oven door.
                     After a few quick tries with his keys he deftly
                     undoes the padlock and throws the door open.
                     To his amazement there is no cavity there
                     now. He is faced with a solid wall as the door
                     swings back. The oven is bricked up.*)

ALBERT   (*in astonishment*) Well, I'm blowed!

                     (*Blackout.*)

                              Scene Two

*The next day - Sunday - is bright and clear after the rain.
Now that the curtains are drawn, iron bars are visible on the
inside of the windows.* LOUISA'S *telescope is standing on the
dresser.* EMILY'S *shells are still on the piano. The bake-oven
door is closed again. There is a small fire burning on the
hearth. The candles are out.*

It is shortly after noon.

ALBERT, *in his shirt sleeves, with a towel round his neck, is
busy lathering his face. Shaving materials are on the table.*
LUCY *enters from the kitchen with a small wall-mirror which
she brings to* ALBERT.

ALBERT   (*taking it*) Ta. We'll prop it up here, shall we?
                (*He puts it on the window sill.*) Is this your
                mirror, Lucy?

LUCY   It's from my bedroom.

ALBERT   Sees a lot of pretty scenery, that mirror —
                doesn't it?

LUCY   You are awful, aren't you?

ALBERT   So are you - if you're honest with yourself.
                It's given you quite a lift-up, my coming back
                — hasn't it?

LUCY   It's given me a lot of extra work.

ALBERT   Nice work, though.

                (*He tries to kiss her but she eludes him.*)

LUCY   Here! I've washed my face this morning,
                thank you.

ALBERT   D'ye know, Lucy, you've blossomed out since
                I was here last. Quite the young lady, aren't
                you?

LUCY   I can't say you've improved.

ALBERT   Oh, come off it. You'd better make the best of
                me while I *am* here. I may be going abroad
                shortly.

LUCY   No! Are you going abroad? Where?

ALBERT   I don't know. America probably. Or India.

LUCY   Oh, I *should* like to see India.

ALBERT   (*stropping his razor, which is of the "cut-
                throat" type*) Would you? Well, if you're nice
                to me, I'd see if I can't find you a cosy little
                corner down among the boilers when I stow
                aboard. It might help to melt you.

LUCY   It'd take more than boilers to do that.

ALBERT   Don't be so full of back answers. You'll eat
                your words one day.

LUCY   Oh, shall I, Mr Know-All?

ALBERT   I've a good mind to make you swallow 'em now.

LUCY   (*as he advances towards her*) You'll get a
                black eye if you try anything with me. You
                keep your distance.

ALBERT   You forget I've got a razor in my hand. Just
                for that I think I'll have a kiss now, after all -
                soap or no soap.

LUCY   I'll scream the place down if you touch me.

ALBERT   (*cheery*) If you do I'll slit your gizzard. Now,
                come along, be a nice little girl. You've got
                to go through it, you know.

LUCY   Well, you'll have to catch me, then!

ALBERT   That's a bargain. (*He puts down the razor,
                chases her and corners her on the settle
                where he kisses her soundly.*) You little devil,
                pretending all this time you were an iceberg.

LUCY   I oughtn't to let you do this.

ALBERT   What do you think lips were made for?

LUCY   Leading respectable young girls astray - yours
                were.

                (*He tries again.*)

                No. You've done quite enough for one Sunday
                morning. My face is all over soap. (*She takes
                the towel from round his neck and wipes her
                face.*) Now, you get on with your shaving.
                Miss Emily will come down and catch us.

ALBERT   Oh, I'd forgotten she's not at chapel.

LUCY	And you wouldn't like me to be sent home, would you?
ALBERT	(*now shaving hard*) You bet I wouldn't. No, don't go. Stay and talk to me.
LUCY	I've got the breakfast things to wash.
ALBERT	That can wait. I'll come and help you wash up later.
LUCY	I don't see you doing much washing up.
ALBERT	What have you got these bars over the window for?
LUCY	To keep out wicked boys like you.
ALBERT	No, seriously. I don't remember 'em when I was here before.
LUCY	Miss Creed had them put up after Miss Fiske went away.
ALBERT	Seems a funny idea.
LUCY	Your aunts are all a bit funny.
ALBERT	That's a fact. She's a nice old dear, Miss Fiske. Quite a good sport, isn't she?
LUCY	She's always finding fault. But she is human.
ALBERT	How long's she been away?
LUCY	Nearly two months.
ALBERT	Where's she gone?
LUCY	I don't know. I didn't know she was going even. She never said anything about it.
ALBERT	Why? Did she just walk out, then?
LUCY	I don't know. I was away on my holiday. When I came back she'd gone. Funny, wasn't it?
ALBERT	Perhaps she and Aunt Ellen had a row.

LUCY

Couldn't have been that, could it? Because then it would have been for your aunt to go. It's Miss Fiske's house.

ALBERT

Yes. You're right there. She'll turn up one day.

LUCY

Well, Miss Ellen can't be expecting her just yet. Because you're to have Miss Fiske's room as long as you're staying. I've just been getting it ready.

ALBERT

(*wiping his face*) There, that's better. I feel a little less like the missing link. Good job Miss Fiske left her razor. I don't suppose my aunts could have lent me one between 'em.

LUCY

I wonder what *she* wants a razor for.

ALBERT

(*slyly*) Corns, I don't think. (*As she turns to go.*) Half a mo. Have you got a bit of black wire?

LUCY

Whatever for?

ALBERT

(*at the bake-oven*) See this padlock? I was fooling about with it last night, and it came open. I couldn't get it shut again.

LUCY

You oughtn't to have done that! That's where Miss Fiske keeps her money.

ALBERT

Oh, no, you're wrong there. Quite wrong, duckie. There's only a wall behind there.

LUCY

That's all you know! It's an old bake-oven.

ALBERT

Bake-oven my foot! (*He opens the door.*) Look!

LUCY

Well I never! It's been bricked up! I wonder when that was done? But it was a bake-oven. Miss Fiske used to call it her safe.

ALBERT

When did you last see it opened?

LUCY   When I was going on my holiday. Miss Fiske
                gave me my money out of it.

ALBERT   If that's where the money used to be kept it
                wouldn't do for it to look as though I'd been
                playing about with it, would it? I mean,
                people think nasty thoughts sometimes, don't
                they?

LUCY   Yes. And sometimes they're right, aren't
                they? (*Taking her mirror and going to the
                kitchen.*) I'll get that wire.

ALBERT   And bring a pair of pliers if you've got 'em.

                (LUCY *goes out.* ALBERT *puts on his coat and
                combs his hair in front of the glass.* LUCY
                returns with some wire and the pliers.)

                Ta. It only wants a small bit. I don't want it
                to show.

                (*He takes the wire and the pliers and quickly
                adjusts the padlock.*)

LUCY   You are clever with your fingers!

ALBERT   (*as he works*) By the way, is there a flue from
                in there up into the main chimney?

LUCY   Of course not. It's a bake-oven, stupid.

ALBERT   I know it is, clever! Then it must be all air-
                tight behind there?

LUCY   Of course it's air-tight.

ALBERT   I wonder why anyone should want to brick up
                a place like that.

LUCY   (*artfully*) I know why. Miss Fiske probably
                put her jewels in there before she went away.
                They were always playing about with bricks,
                and pulling the walls down. She didn't want
                to take any chances — not even with your aunt.

ALBERT   I dare say you're right. I wouldn't mind
having a peep at those jewels.

LUCY   Oh, so that's why you wanted to know if it
had a flue of it's own? You'd have soon been
on the roof with a fishing line, *I* know!

ALBERT   (*artfully*) If I read *you* rightly you wouldn't
mind the feel of some of Miss Fiske's jewels
round your neck.

LUCY   I never thought of such a thing.

ALBERT   Be honest. I bet you've envied 'em.

LUCY   Well, it is a bit of a waste - pearls round an
old woman's throat.

ALBERT   Pity one needs a pick-axe to get at 'em. A
nice pair of earrings might take you and me to
Australia.

        (*There is a sharp double knock on the front
door.* ALBERT *is terrified. He tiptoes to the
stairway where he stands on the bottom step
in the shadow ready to make a bolt for it.*
LUCY *watches him in astonishment.*)

        (*in a whisper*) Who's that? Don't open it. See
who it is. And come and tell me first.

LUCY   (*she looks out of the window and then comes
to him*) It's the post.

        (*At the same time a letter is thrust under the
door.*)

ALBERT   (*relieved*) Oh.

LUCY   (*retrieving the letter*) He's gone. Here's the
letter. It's for Miss Fiske from her bank.

ALBERT   How do you know?

        (*He takes the letter.*)

LUCY   There's the crest on the envelope. Why were
            you so scared?

ALBERT   I wasn't scared. I'd forgotten you had a
            Sunday post.

LUCY   Don't tell me you weren't scared! You were
            frightened out of your skin. Are you in
            trouble?

ALBERT   We all make mistakes, don't we?

LUCY   I believe you're hiding from the police.

ALBERT   Supposing I am? You wouldn't think any the
            less of me for that, would you?

LUCY   That depends.

            (*He takes her in his arms and kisses her again.*)

            Look out! Someone's coming!

            (*They separate hastily as* EMILY *comes
            downstairs.* LUCY *flies.*)

ALBERT   Good morning, Aunt Emily. How is it you're
            not at chapel?

EMILY   I had a headache.

ALBERT   Oh no! Aunt Ellen's cognac too much for you?

EMILY   It wasn't Ellen's. It was Miss Fiske's. Ellen
            really oughtn't to have given it to you.
            Unless, of course, she bought it.

ALBERT   Don't say Miss Fiske would have begrudged it
            to us.

EMILY   (*by the piano, at her tray*) I don't know. I
            never liked her.

ALBERT   By the way, there's a letter just come for her.
            It wants re-addressing. Shall I do it? It'll save
            trouble.

EMILY   You'd better not touch that, Albert. Ellen
                 might not like it. Besides, I don't know her
                 address.

                 (ALBERT *puts the letter on the dresser.* EMILY
                 takes up her tray.)

EMILY   I'll just put my glue down by the fire here.
                 It'll be ready when I come back. I'm going
                 for a walk.

ALBERT   Where are you going?

EMILY   I'm going down to look at the floods. The
                 dykes always overflow in these big rains.

ALBERT   Don't run away, my dear. I don't often have
                 the chance of a tete-a-tete with the handsome
                 one of the family.

EMILY   (*sitting down*) I think you're making fun of
                 me, Albert.

ALBERT   Now would I do a thing like that? (*Chattily.*)
                 This is a very comfortable house you three are
                 living in. Jolly sight better than your lodgings
                 in Kennington!

EMILY   Yes. They were horrid.

ALBERT   What's going to happen to you when Miss
                 Fiske comes back? Will she let you stay on?

EMILY   She isn't coming back.

ALBERT   Isn't she? Why not?

EMILY   Ellen's bought the house.

ALBERT   Go on!

EMILY   Oh, yes. It's quite true. But it's a secret. Ellen
                 made me swear on the Bible I wouldn't tell
                 anyone. But you're one of the family. So it's
                 different.

ALBERT	Why did Aunt Ellen want to keep it so secret?
EMILY	I don't know. It was all done in a great hurry. Aunt Louisa and I were sent out for a long drive, and when we came back it was all over and Miss Fiske had gone. You won't tell Ellen I told you, will you?
ALBERT	No. We'll make that our little secret, shall we?
EMILY	Yes. It's rather fun to have a secret Ellen doesn't know anything about. She always thinks she's the clever one. But she isn't - not always. I'll tell you another secret, Albert. Oh, no, I won't.
ALBERT	Why not? Didn't you say I was one of the family?
EMILY	I think Ellen's done something that's not quite right.
ALBERT	Why?
EMILY	Because she's looked so worried lately. And I've heard her walking about the house very late at night.
ALBERT	That's nothing. That might be indigestion.
EMILY	Yes, it might be. But I don't think it is. When it gets dark she lights those horrid little candles. She never used to do anything like that. It's only since Miss Fiske's been gone. Do you think, Albert, she hasn't really bought the house?
ALBERT	Well, if she hasn't, it's rather a large article to steal, isn't it?
EMILY	There might be ways of getting it.
ALBERT	What sort of ways?
EMILY	(*after a pause*) I don't know, Albert. I haven't thought.

(*There is a light knock at the front door. He darts to the window.*)

ALBERT   Why, it's an old nun! Where's she blown from?

EMILY   She'll be from the Priory. It's down the lane. Will you open the door to her, Albert? I don't like nuns.

(ALBERT *opens the door.* SISTER THERESA *enters. She has a gallon can of oil with her.*)

THERESA   Oh, good morning. Is Miss Ellen Creed in?

ALBERT   No. I'm her nephew. She's gone over to, where was it, Aunt Emily?

EMILY   The Little Bethel at Cooling.

ALBERT   (*to* THERESA) Ah, that's it. Chapel, you know. Can I do anything?

THERESA   The Reverend Mother's sent me up to repay this oil which you lent us last night. The cart which was bringing our supply got waterlogged. They couldn't get beyond the farm. So they left it there and Mr Braiden kindly brought it up this morning. The Reverend Mother wanted you to have it at once.

ALBERT   (*taking it*) I'll take it through.

EMILY   (*rising*) No. I'll go, Albert. I know where it's kept.

(*She takes the can and, without a glance at* THERESA *goes out into the kitchen.* THERESA *produces an envelope.*)

THERESA   And, as I was coming, the Reverend Mother thought I might save a journey and bring the rent for Miss Fiske's field - if Miss Creed doesn't mind taking it on a Sunday.

ALBERT   (*receiving it*) Oh, bless you, I've no objection. The better the day the better the deed. I'll give it her when she comes in.

THERESA   Tell her not to trouble with the receipt till the next time someone's passing our way.

ALBERT   (*casually*) Did you know Miss Fiske well - who owned this place?

THERESA   Oh yes. She still does, doesn't she?

ALBERT   Oh, yes.

THERESA   We all know her at the convent. She's a dear friend of ours.

ALBERT   I've only met her once. She seemed a very agreeable lady. I suppose you've no idea when she'll be back?

THERESA   No. As a matter of fact, we didn't know she was going away. The Reverend Mother was quite surprised when she heard she'd gone. And I think she's been a little hurt that Miss Fiske hasn't written to her. But perhaps I oughtn't to say that.

ALBERT   Why not? It's a free country.

THERESA   (*preparing to go*) By the way, Mr Braiden tells us that the main roads from Rochester and Gravesend are under water by the marshes so we're quite cut off. And may be for some days.

ALBERT   (*secretly delighted*) That won't worry us.

THERESA   No, but it's just as well to know, isn't it?

ALBERT   Rather. Thanks for the tip.

THERESA   You're welcome. Good morning.

(*She goes, shutting the door.* ALBERT *stands, shaking the envelope to his ear. He realises there is money in it. He looks, for him, very thoughtful. It is as though a vague idea were taking shape in his mind.* LUCY *enters, from the kitchen.*)

LUCY

Miss Emily told me to tell you she's gone out for her walk. She went out the back way. She didn't want to meet the Sister again.

ALBERT

Narrow-minded old parrot! Here, just a minute, ducks. Got a kettle boiling out there?

LUCY

Why?

ALBERT

Never you mind. Have you got one?

LUCY

Well, perhaps I have. What do you want it for?

ALBERT

Bring it in here then I'll show you.

(LUCY *goes into the kitchen.* ALBERT *puts the nun's letter on the bureau.* LUCY *returns with a steaming kettle.*)

ALBERT

(*indicating the table*) That's right. Now put it down there.

LUCY

You can't stand it on the table!

ALBERT

No. I know! (*Going to the piano and taking up a score.*) This bit of music. Stand it on here.

LUCY

Oh, you mustn't do that. That's Miss Fiske's.

ALBERT

(*reading it*) "The Mikado. From her friend Rutland Barrington." Oh, I've seen that before. No we'd better not use that. That's special. (*Taking up another.*) Here. "The Elijah." He'll do. He's used to heat in the desert.

LUCY

(*putting down the kettle on Mendelssohn*) What do you want to do?

ALBERT

(*taking the bank's letter from the dresser*) Lucy, I've got a notion something's a bit wrong and I want to have a look at something.

LUCY

What?

ALBERT	This letter that came from the bank for Miss Fiske this morning.
LUCY	Yes, what about it?
ALBERT	I'm going to have a look at what's inside.
LUCY	You can't go opening other people's letters.
ALBERT	(*slyly*) Did you like Miss Fiske?
LUCY	Yes. She's a kind lady. She's been very generous to me.
ALBERT	Yes. She was very good to me, too. She got me out of a bit of trouble, and I owe her a debt of gratitude.
LUCY	Well, it's a funny way to pay for it to open her private letters!
ALBERT	It might not be. I'm a little worried. Hold the lid, will you?
LUCY	If you're going to open that, I'm not going to be a party to it.
ALBERT	(*removing the kettle lid and holding the envelope in the steam*) All right, then. You needn't stay if you're squeamish. You clear off into the kitchen. But I don't mind telling you I'm going to have a look at it. (*Pause.*) If there's nothing startling in it - well, we've done no harm, have we? We can seal it up again. On the other hand, if there is something, we're doing a service to Miss Fiske, aren't we?
LUCY	You'd argue the hind leg off a donkey.
ALBERT	I knew you'd see my way.
LUCY	Hurry up, then. They'll be back from chapel soon.
	(*He has opened it now.*)
	Well, what's it say?

ALBERT   (*reading*) "Dear Madam, re your letter
                instructing us to forward the amount of the
                enclosed cheque in five pound notes to the
                payee, your signature appears to differ from
                that with which we are acquainted. I shall be
                obliged if you will kindly confirm the same
                by signing it afresh in your usual manner."
                (*Looking at the attached cheque.*) It's for fifty
                quid. (*Then he whistles.*) Do you notice the date?

LUCY   (*reading it over his shoulder*) November the
                fourteenth.

ALBERT   I thought she went away in September?

LUCY   But she may have written the cheque from
                wherever she is, mayn't she?

ALBERT   But why have they written back to her here?
                And do you notice who the cheque's made
                payable to?

LUCY   "Miss Ellen Creed". Well, what of it? I expect
                it's the housekeeping money.

ALBERT   Yes, you're probably right. Well, it's a dead
                end, anyhow. Now we'd better cover up our
                tracks, hadn't we? (*He picks up the glue pot.*)
                Just dip your forefinger in Aunt Emily's glue,
                will you?

LUCY   I'm not doing anything about it. I've had no
                hand in this.

ALBERT   Haven't you? (*He suddenly seizes her hand
                and puts a finger in the glue.*) Now then, seal
                it up.

LUCY   You are a filthy pig!

                (*She seals the envelope reluctantly.*)

ALBERT   (*standing the letter back on the dresser*) Now,
                we'll put it up here, and I'll hand it to Aunt

Ellen later. That'll give it a chance to dry.
And don't forget - you're in this as deep as me.

LUCY I wish you'd never come here. There's
something about you that frightens me out of
my life.

ALBERT I don't mind telling you I frighten myself
sometimes.

LUCY I don't know what's come over me. You seem
to mesmerize me. You won't give me away to
Miss Creed, will you?

ALBERT Not so long as you keep your mouth shut
about me. (*A noise outside attracts him. He
peers through the window.*) Hullo! Here come
the performing seals! Quick - take the kettle
into the kitchen.

(LUCY *picks up the kettle and hurries out.*
ALBERT *respectfully opens the front door to*
ELLEN *and* LOUISA *who enter. They are in their
Sunday best.*)

ALBERT Hullo, aunts. Had a nice pray?

ELLEN (*grimly*) There's no need to be facetious, Albert.

LOUISA It would have done you good to come too,
Albert. It was quite exciting. The minister
was telling us all about Hell. You would have
enjoyed the picture he drew of fire and
brimstone and the lost people burning in the pit.

ALBERT Oh, I've had quite a good time, thanks -
smelling the bit of dead bullock sizzling on
the stove in Aunt Ellen's kitchen.

ELLEN That's very irreverent. You shouldn't joke
about such things.

ALBERT I'm afraid I can't take Hell all that seriously
Auntie. I don't hold with these preachers
hollering themselves hoarse about eternal fire.

After all, if there is such a place, no one's
ever come back from it. So where do they get
all their geographical details from?

ELLEN   (*with deep, if concerned, feeling*) Hell's like
the Kingdom of Heaven. It's within.

ALBERT   (*struck by her manner, but jauntily*) I bet you
read that in a book somewhere, Auntie.
What's an innocent old cup of tea like you
ever done to know anything about Hell?

LOUISA   But, Albert, Aunt Ellen's clever. She knows
about all sorts of things. She may know about
Hell, too.

ALBERT   You don't say! We'll have to christen her
"Hell-Fire Ellen".

LOUISA   (*going into fits of laughter*) Oh, he does say
funny things, doesn't he? "Hell-Fire Ellen!"
Ho! Ho! I must tell Emily!

ALBERT   (*he is now at the fireplace and takes up the
"slice"*) Yes, of course! And that explains
why she keeps a pitchfork handy. To help
jolly old Lucifer turn over the fry in his oven.

               (*He pokes* LOUISA *playfully with the "slice."*
               ELLEN *turns on him in a fury and grips his
               wrist.*)

ELLEN   Put that down! I won't have you talking like
this in my house on a Sunday.

ALBERT   (*complying in feigned surprise*) It's all right,
Auntie. I was only trying to bring a little
sunshine into your lives. You want digging
out of yourselves. You three lead such a
walled-up existence here, you don't realise
how the rest of the people in the world live.

ELLEN   Perhaps we know a little more than you give
us credit for.

LOUISA   Yes, Albert. Aunt Emily and I may be a little old-fashioned. But Aunt Ellen's very up-to-date.

ALBERT   (*taking up the nun's letter*) By the way, Auntie, somebody called while you were out - asking for a Miss Fiske.

ELLEN   What! Who was it?

ALBERT   One of your religious friends down the road. She gave me this. She just said it was for Miss Fiske and would I give it to you. (*Rattling the letter*.) It's got money in it.

ELLEN   Very well. I'll take it.

        (*She takes it and puts it into her bag*.)

ALBERT   (*innocently*) Who is this Miss Fiske everybody's always mentioning?

ELLEN   Oh, she's just someone who used to live here.

LOUISA   She didn't like Emily and me. She was horrid. We were so glad when she went away.

ELLEN   Hadn't you better go upstairs, Louisa, and take your things off?

LOUISA   Oh, but I do like being with Albert, Ellen. He does say such funny things.

ELLEN   You won't want to sit about in the house in your best all day.

LOUISA   No, I shan't, shall I, Ellen? No, of course.

        (*She trots upstairs.* ELLEN *shuts the stairway door*.)

ELLEN   Albert, I don't want you to mention Miss Fiske again in front of your aunts. They quarrelled and it excites them very much to talk about her.

ALBERT   (*mock penitently*) Oh, I wouldn't like to do
            that. Of course, I won't refer to the subject
            again, Auntie. You see, nobody told me. But,
            I say! How comic - your quarrelling. What did
            you quarrel about, Auntie?

ELLEN   I didn't say that I quarrelled with her.

ALBERT   Oh, then I suppose she's the friend you
            lighted those candles for last night? I see!

ELLEN   Yes. that's right. She's that friend.

ALBERT   You must have been very fond of her. When
            did she die?

ELLEN   Die? Who said she was dead? Who said
            anything about her dying?

ALBERT   I just assumed she was. You don't light
            candles for the living, do you?

ELLEN   Why not?

ALBERT   Well, Catholics don't, do they?

ELLEN   I'm not a Catholic. I thought candles just
            stood for prayer.

ALBERT   Is that so? You may be right. I'm not up in
            the technique. I say - it must have been a
            priceless quarrel. I'd love to have seen it.
            Fancy the old birds driving Miss Fiske out of
            here for good!

ELLEN   We don't know that it is for good. She's away
            on a holiday. She may come back.

ALBERT   Crikey! Is it her room I'm having?

ELLEN   Yes.

ALBERT   What's going to happen to me if she turns up?

ELLEN   I expect you'll be gone by then.

ALBERT   I hope so. I don't fancy many more nights on
            this sofa.

ELLEN	Why? Weren't you comfortable?
ALBERT	Oh, I suppose so. But I didn't sleep too well. (*With a sudden change of tone, quite sincerely and seriously.*) Aunt Ellen, do you believe in ghosts?
ELLEN	No. Of course not.
ALBERT	Neither do I. At least, I thought I didn't. But, d'you know, last night - in the middle of the night, I woke up. I can't describe it, but I had a funny feeling there was someone in the room with me.
ELLEN	That was all that cognac. There are no ghosts in Estuary House.
ALBERT	Well, there aren't any anywhere, are there? (*Suddenly.*) There! Damn, if I haven't got a memory like a sieve.
ELLEN	What have you forgotten?
ALBERT	The other letter. Now where did I put it? Oh, yes. Over here on the dresser. (*He takes down the bank's letter.*) It came by the post. It's another one for Miss Fiske. From a bank. It gave me quite a turn when I saw it was from a bank! If you like to re-address it, I'll take it down to the box. I could do with a breather.
ELLEN	(*taking it*) I'm looking after everything for her while she's away. It may be important. I think I'd better open it, don't you?
ALBERT	Why not - if she wouldn't mind?
	(ALBERT *wanders to the piano, watching her covertly. She opens the letter, and reacts to the contents.*)
ALBERT	That's a nice piano you've got here.
ELLEN	(*absorbed*) What? Oh, yes. I believe it is.

ALBERT   Why, it's a Pleyel! And, by Jove, isn't it
                stylish?

ELLEN   (*sitting at the bureau*) Don't worry me,
                Albert. I must write a note. It's rather urgent.
                I must concentrate.

ALBERT   Don't mind me, Auntie. And you are up-to-
                date! I never expected to find a copy of The
                Mikado here!

                (*He stands turning over the pages of the
                score. Then he saunters over and sits on the
                sofa watching* ELLEN *as she writes. Suddenly
                he begins to whistle "Tit-Willow"* . . . ELLEN
                rises with a little cry.)

ELLEN   Don't do that!

ALBERT   Sorry, Auntie. Didn't mean to interrupt.

ELLEN   It's not that. But I hate that particular tune.

ALBERT   (*as she resumes her writing*) Do you? I'll find
                something cheerier.

                (EMILY *enters from the front door. She is
                carrying some stands of bryony berries which
                she has torn from the hedge.*)

EMILY   I couldn't get down to the marsh. The floods
                were too bad.

ALBERT   (*irreverently*) That's too bad.

                (*She crosses the room and goes upstairs.*)

ALBERT   (*still reading the score*) Ha! Ha! This might
                be you and Emily and Louisa, mightn't it?
                (*He sings in a half-voice*).

                "Three little maids from school are we,
                Pert as a schoolgirl well can be.
                Filled to the brim with girlish glee,
                Three little maids from school."

                (LUCY *looks in from the kitchen.*)

LUCY   Will you be ready for dinner in ten minutes, Miss?

ELLEN   (*blotting and sealing her letter*) Make it a quarter of an hour, Lucy. I've got to run down to the letter-box.

                (LUCY *retires.*)

ALBERT   Let me go for you, Auntie.

ELLEN   Thank you. I'd rather do it myself.

                (*She crosses the room and goes out of the front door.* ALBERT *goes over to the bureau, examines the blotter and tears a sheet from it and then crosses to the kitchen door.*)

ALBERT   (*calling into the kitchen*) Lucy! Bring us back your mirror, will you?

                (*She enters carrying her mirror.*)

                Here. Hold it up, facing the light.

LUCY   I should think you'd have got sick of the sight of your face.

ALBERT   I don't want it for that. I want to read what Aunt Ellen's written to the bank. It's on her blotter, see? The other way about.

LUCY   You oughtn't to do this.

ALBERT   Hold it up.

                (*She stands facing the window and holding up the glass. He holds the blotting paper to it and reads in the mirror, but with some slight difficulty.*)

                "Dear Sir, Cheque - something - quite correct. Owing to a sprained hand there may be a discrepancy in some of my cheques lately signed. Yours - something- Leonora Fiske."

LUCY   "Leonora Fiske"? Your aunt's signed "Leonora Fiske"? What's it mean, Albert?

ALBERT	(*laying the blotting paper thoughtfully on the table*) Shouldn't like to say.
LUCY	(*suddenly*) I know! It means she's pretending to be Miss Fiske and stealing money from her bank!
ALBERT	That's what it looks like.
LUCY	(*putting down the mirror casually on the table so that it covers the blotting paper*) I means she's a thief - like you.
ALBERT	Here!
LUCY	But she's taking an awful risk! There'll be the deuce to pay when Miss Fiske comes back.
ALBERT	Supposing she isn't coming back? Supposing she's dead on her holiday? Supposing Aunt Ellen's the only one who knows?
LUCY	You can't die and only one person know.
ALBERT	No, you can't, can you? But somehow I don't think the old canary'd risk stealing from her unless she knew she wasn't coming back.
LUCY	And, I say! I've just thought of something!
ALBERT	What's that?
LUCY	When I was getting Miss Fiske's room ready for you this morning what d'you think I found tucked away in the cupboard?
ALBERT	What?
LUCY	Her best wig.
ALBERT	Oh? Did she wear a wig?
LUCY	Lord, yes. She was nearly bald. She looked a scream when you took in her morning cup of tea. Why didn't she take it with her? She

rather fancies herself, you know. Why should she go away in her old one?

ALBERT   What about her clothes? Has she taken her best clothes?

LUCY   I never thought to look. But I couldn't have told. She's got chests full of dresses, and they're all locked.

ALBERT   When I get into the room we'll have a look. The locks won't worry me. And you give me some idea what's missing.

LUCY   Why are you so curious about all this?

ALBERT   Supposing Miss Fiske is dead. Supposing Aunt Ellen is tapping the funds. It might be a lifetime before anyone finds out. Why should the old canary reap all the benefit? There might be some nice pickings in it for you and me. There might even be India or Australia in it - if we play our cards.

LUCY   You'd tempt Old Nick himself, wouldn't you?

ALBERT   You needn't help me if you don't want to. I can do it all on my own. But if I'm right, and I can pull it off you might do worse than join forces with me. You don't dislike me, do you?

LUCY   I ought to . . .

ALBERT   But you don't. I don't dislike you either. I think you're one of the smartest little pieces I've set eyes on.

(*He kisses her.*)

LUCY   (*in a low voice*) I'll help.

ALBERT   Good girl.

LUCY   What do you want me to do?

ALBERT   I'll have to think out something.

LUCY   I don't want to do anything mean or underhand.

ALBERT   I wouldn't ask you, would I? But we've got to get proof. You keep your peepers open. You watch. I'll watch. And keep your ears close to keyholes - listen.

LUCY   All right. There's plenty of chances 'cos they're always talking nineteen to the dozen.

ALBERT   Listen to Aunt Ellen. She's the one.

(*A hissing noise is heard from the kitchen.*)

LUCY   Beggar me ! There's something boiling over! Come out with me. We can talk in the kitchen.

(*They hurry off.* ELLEN *enters by the front door. She comes into the room, takes off her bonnet and lays it on the table. Then she sees the mirror. She picks it up, glances at it in a puzzled way, then sees the blotting paper. She looks suspiciously towards the kitchen. Then she examines the blotting paper and, with a fierce exclamation crumples it up and throws it in the fire.* LUCY *enters. Her movement suggests that she has been coming for the mirror. On seeing* ELLEN *she hesitates.*)

ELLEN   (*turning, and in a voice with rage behind it*) What's your mirror doing in here, Lucy?

LUCY   Mr Albert borrowed it - for his shaving.

ELLEN   Oh, I see. Well, take it back with you. And serve dinner.

(LUCY *picks up the mirror and departs.* ELLEN *goes to the gong, takes the beater and begins to strike the bronze. She is still banging as the lights fade.*)

ACT THREE

Scene One

It is the following Wednesday night. The lamps are lighted and the fire is burning brightly. The curtains, however, are not drawn, and the moonlight streams through the windows. The candles in front of the Virgin are not lighted.

Sitting around the table are ALBERT, LOUISA *and* LUCY. *They are playing a game of three-handed cribbage. The cognac bottle and a glass are in front of* ALBERT. EMILY *is on the sofa with her beloved tray of shells on a little table in front of her. She is busy working.*

ALBERT	(*scoring a game, to* LOUISA) You owe me five farthings, my bell of St Martins.
LOUISA	I'm sure you're cheating me, Albert. I thought I'd won.
EMILY	You shouldn't play for money. You know it's wrong.
LOUISA	But Father always used to play crib for farthings. Don't you remember, Emily? There can't be any harm in farthings.
EMILY	Father could afford to play for farthings.
ALBERT	Now, just one more go - my old bell of Bow.
LOUISA	Oh! What will you call me next, Albert? I don't think we'd better play any more. Ellen will be back soon.
ALBERT	(*dealing*) Frightened of being put in the corner? All right, you naughty girl. I'll take the blame. By the way, does anyone know where Aunt Ellen's been?
EMILY	She never tells us where she goes. We're nobody.
LOUISA	I think she's gone to Rochester on business.

ALBERT   What business?

LOUISA   I think it must be to buy something for the
            chickens to eat. Because there's not much left
            in their bin. And she said it was important.

EMILY   I don't think it had anything to do with
            chickens. She looked so determined.

ALBERT   I know! She's gone to get some dog collars
            for the ducks.

LOUISA   (*laughing shrilly*) Isn't he silly, Emily?

ALBERT   Silly? Look at the way they've been straying
            away since the floods. Chain 'em up! I think
            it's a grand idea.

EMILY   The floods have gone down. They didn't last
            long this time.

ALBERT   Well, let's get on with our ducks and dresses
            here. Now, Lucy, show us your paces. Time
            you won something. You'll be lucky this deal.

LUCY   Luck doesn't come into it, playing with you.

ALBERT   Here we are. Now throw out our crib. Come
            on, Auntie. You *are* a slow coach.

LOUISA   Don't rush me, Albert. You confuse me.
            (*Putting out her crib.*) But I think that'll be
            all right.

ALBERT   Right. Start off. (*They each play a card
            calling out its value as they go and, marking
            up the various points.*) Nine.

LUCY   Eleven.

LOUISA   Fifteen. (*Marking up two on the board.*)
            That's fifteen-two.

ALBERT   (*marking up two also*) And a pair. That's
            seventeen.

LUCY	Twenty seven.
ALBERT	Thirty-on. That's two to me.
	(*He marks it up.*)
LOUISA	You moved the peg more than two, Albert.
ALBERT	(*ignoring this*) Now wait a minute. (*He scores his own hand.*) Fifteen-two, fifteen-four, fifteen-six and a pair's eight, sequence twelve and one for his nob thirteen! (*To* LOUISA.) I'll have to take you down a peg, my charmer.
LOUISA	(*as he does so*) Oh, Albert! Now I *have* caught you cheating. You've muddled up all the pegs and I've gone right down to the bottom again. I won't play any more. I don't mind a little cheating, but you mustn't cheat every time.
LUCY	I should ask him for all your farthings back, Miss Louisa.
LOUISA	Albert, please give me back all my farthings.
ALBERT	(*rattling the coppers*) All right, my darling. Here you are. I wouldn't rob you. I'll tell you what. I'll toss you double or quits.
LOUISA	I don't know what that means.
ALBERT	If you win, we're quits. If you lose, you pay me double. (*Tossing a coin.*) Come on. Call.
EMILY	Don't, Louisa. He's up to no good.
LOUISA	What do I care?
ALBERT	Heads or tails.
LOUISA	Heads, then.
ALBERT	(*looking at the coin and it is apparent from his face that he has really lost the toss*) Tails it is. You pay me double.

LOUISA   But I haven't got double. You've got all my
                farthings.

ALBERT   All right, Auntie. We'll chalk it up. And in
                the meantime I'll loan you back your
                farthings at ten per cent per annum.

                (*He tips the coins into her lap.*)

EMILY   You're too full of tricks, Albert. You'll be
                behind bars one day.

ALBERT   What's your name? Mrs Job? And, as for bars
                we're more or less behind 'em now, aren't
                we? I wonder why they're there. I suppose
                they've been up for hundreds of years.

LOUISA   Oh, no. They're quite new. Ellen put them there.

ALBERT   Did she, now? You don't say!

LUCY   My goodness! That reminds me. I've
                forgotten to shut up.

                (*She has risen and closes the curtains.*)

EMILY   Ellen's afraid of someone breaking in.

ALBERT   (*mock dramatically*) Perhaps she's a miser.
                Perhaps she comes down here in the middle of
                the night and counts her gold.

EMILY   She does come down here in the middle of the
                night. But I don't think she counts her gold.

LUCY   (*still at the window*) Here's the cart. Here is
                Miss Ellen. I'll go and bring in her tray. (*She
                goes out into the kitchen. The cart is heard
                stopping.*)

ALBERT   (*opening the front door*) Hullo, Aunt! Had a
                nice trip?

                (ELLEN *enters. She is warmly wrapped up.*)

ELLEN   It was bitterly cold.

ALBERT   Shall I take the driver out a glass of
                  something?

ELLEN   (*dryly*) Certainly. If it's not just an excuse for
                  having one yourself.

ALBERT   (*pouring out some cognac*) There's not
                  enough or that. Aunt Louisa's swigged nearly
                  the whole bottle.

LOUISA   Oh, Albert - you story! I haven't taken even a
                  sip. I haven't been asked to.

ALBERT   (*teasing her*) You wicked old gambler!

                  (*The sound of the cart can be heard getting
                  ready to pull away and he runs out of the
                  front door with a tumbler.*)

                  Hi! Driver! Wait a minute!

ELLEN   (*closing the front door*) What have you been
                  doing?

LOUISA   Lucy came in and we played a game of crib.
                  Of course Albert cheated. But it was rather
                  fun watching him cheat.

ELLEN   I want you two to go up to bed. I want to
                  speak to Albert alone.

EMILY   I don't want to go to bed.

ELLEN   Well, go up to your room anyway.

                  (EMILY *begins to pack up her work very sullenly.*)

                  What have you been talking about while I've
                  been out, Louisa?

LOUISA   Albert's been making us laugh.

ELLEN   He never talks to you, does he, about Miss Fiske?

LOUISA   Miss Fiske, Ellen? No! Why should he?

ELLEN   (*searchingly*) And you've neither of you told
             him anything about my buying the house,
             have you?

LOUISA   Oh, no, Ellen! Don't you remember you made
             us swear on the Bible we wouldn't?

ELLEN   (*grimly*) I remember.

EMILY   But it wasn't the Bible, Ellen. Did you know
             that? It was a Roman Catholic prayer book. I
             found that out afterwards. So it doesn't count.
             We could tell who we liked, couldn't we?

ELLEN   (*almost beside herself with nervous anger*) If I
             ever find out that either of you breathes a
             word to a soul about my buying the house I'll
             pack you both back to London straight away.
             And I won't send you another penny!

LOUISA   (*beginning to whimper*) Oh, Ellen!

EMILY   (*with an oblique glance*) I'm not going to tell
             anyone, Ellen.

             (ALBERT *returns.*)

LOUISA   Good night, Albert. We're going to bed. Ellen
             thinks it's time we went.

ALBERT   (*to* ELLEN) You've missed your vocation,
             Auntie. You ought to have been a school
             marm. Don't you put up with it, girls. Don't
             you let her bully you.

LOUISA   He is a tease, isn't he, Ellen?

ELLEN   (*with a direct look at* ALBERT) I'm beginning
             to think he's not quite so harmless as that.

EMILY   All the same, Albert's right. You *ought* to
             have been a school marm, Ellen.

LOUISA   (*at the foot of the stairs now*) But it is nice
             having him here! Do you know what he called
             me? The old bell of Bow! (*She cackles with*

laughter.) It's out of that game we used to play when we were children. "'When will you pay me?', said the bell of Old Bailey. 'I do not know,' said the old bell of Bow.''

(*They disappear round the bend of the stairs.* ELLEN *comes to* ALBERT. *You can see that her manner to him has changed completely. She regards him as a dangerous enemy.*)

ELLEN   You've been exciting them again. It's too bad of you. I can't trust you out of my sight.

ALBERT   (*innocently*) Oh, Auntie! What have *I* done?

ELLEN   I'm never sure *what* you may do.

ALBERT   There's not much I could do, is there? After all, this isn't a bank. You haven't got any locks to pick, have you?

(*Her lips set tightly.* LUCY *enters with a tray on which are a glass of milk and a plate of sandwiches.*)

LUCY   I've brought your supper, Miss.

ELLEN   Put it down on the table. And then you can go to bed, Lucy. I'm just going up to wash and take off my things. And wait here, Albert. I've got something to say to you.

(*And she goes brusquely up the stairs.*)

ALBERT   She's on the rampage tonight. There's a nasty look in her eye.

LUCY   Wonder where she's been all day?

ALBERT   I asked the driver. He picked her up at Rochester off the London train.

LUCY   London? Has she been to London?

ALBERT   Yes. I can't understand it. She'd no call to go rushing up there seeing that the fifty pounds

came through from the bank yesterday.
You're sure that's what that registered letter
was?

LUCY   I told you. It was a bank envelope. I took it
            in. I signed for it. Then I watched her through
            the crack of the door. She took out the bundle
            of notes and counted 'em twice very
            carefully. There were ten of them.

ALBERT   Ten five pound notes. I wonder if she means
            to do a bolt. There's nothing for it, Lucy.
            We'll have to try out that plan of mine
            tonight.

LUCY   But supposing it doesn't come off?

ALBERT   Then there's no harm done, is there?

LUCY   I keep telling you, Albert. I don't like it. It's
            risky. It might lose me my place.

ALBERT   Don't be silly. I'll see you through. I'll take
            all the blame. I'll say it was just a practical
            joke of mine to scare the old girls. There's no
            reason why she shouldn't swallow that. She
            knows I'm always codding them. I shall be
            with you. I'll tell you when to come in. Now,
            you will be a darling and go through with this
            for me, Lucy, won't you?

LUCY   (coming to him affectionately) I can't refuse
            you anything now, can I?

ALBERT   (lightly) You're a daisy. You'll be all right.
            All you've got to do is to keep thinking of
            when we'll be married.

LUCY   You'll never go back on me, will you? You're
            not just making use of me?

ALBERT   I've told you. I'm mad about you. (Softly.)
            Haven't I shown you? (Then quickly.) Sssh.
            She's coming down. You get to your room.
            You've got the paraphernalia, haven't you?

LUCY   It's all ready.

       (*She scurries out.* ELLEN *comes downstairs.
       There is a look on her face which shows she is
       ready to give battle.*)

ALBERT (*jauntily*) Well, Auntie, where's your cane?
       From the way you spoke I thought you were
       going to take down my breeches and give me
       a dozen.

ELLEN Don't you wish you *could* pay for your
       misdeeds that way?

ALBERT You take me too seriously, you know. Half
       the time I'm only fooling.

ELLEN One has to take a thief seriously.

ALBERT (*with a shrug*) Oh, come Auntie! We don't
       want to go all over that again, do we? I'm not
       proud of myself. (*With a swift glance.*) We're
       all miserable sinners, aren't we? You used to
       tell me that often enough when I was a little
       boy. I'm not going about in sackcloth and
       ashes for the rest of my life!

ELLEN (*beginning to toy with her supper*) I've been
       to London today.

ALBERT (*with interest*) Have you? Why didn't you tell
       us? You are a dark horse. What, have you
       been on the spree?

ELLEN No. I've been on your account. I've been to a
       shipping company.

ALBERT (*wide eyed*) A shipping company — on my
       account?

ELLEN Yes. I've bought your passage to Canada.

ALBERT (*up in arms*) But I don't want to go to Canada.

ELLEN	(*coldly*) I don't think you've very much choice, have you?
ALBERT	(*half jauntily this time*) I'm quite happy here for the time being.
ELLEN	(*very directly*) I'm not quite happy having you here.
ALBERT	But I thought we'd agreed. I was to lie low till the Gravesend business blew over. Time enough for a passage abroad in a month or so.
ELLEN	I've changed my mind.
ALBERT	Well, I think you might have discussed it with me first.
ELLEN	I didn't see any need. I'm paying the piper.
ALBERT	But what's made you change your mind?
ELLEN	Well, in the first place, you play the fool so much with Louisa and Emily that you'll have them chattering about your being here. And you know what that'll mean. The wrong sort of word to the tradesmen or the nuns and we shall have the police down on us. And I can't do with any scandal here.
ALBERT	(*protestingly*) Oh, but isn't that a bit thin? They're not very difficult to keep an eye on.
ELLEN	You forget Emily goes for long walks. You don't know who she talks to.
ALBERT	But surely there's more to it than that, Auntie? There must be!
ELLEN	Yes. There's Lucy. She's even more dangerous than your aunts.
ALBERT	Oh, Lucy won't give me away.
ELLEN	(*catching at this*) Are you in a position to be sure?

ALBERT	(*very surprised*) What do you mean?
ELLEN	You know well enough what I mean. You wouldn't mind adding Lucy to your conquests, would you?
ALBERT	(*with exaggerated innocence*) It never so much as occurred to me. I've hardly noticed the girl.
ELLEN	Don't lie, Albert. I've watched you whispering together. I saw the way you eyed her the first evening you came. I've seen her setting her cap at you ever since. I'm not going to have that sort of thing going on under my roof!
ALBERT	Well, all I can say, Auntie is - it must be your mind. We're as innocent as the driven snow.
ELLEN	(*with suppressed rage*) You hateful little hypocrite!
ALBERT	Can't one have a joke and a bit of a lark with a girl without being accused of ruining her?
ELLEN	(*sharply*) I never said you'd ruined her. Have you? Am I a little behindhand in sending you away?
ALBERT	(*protesting once more*) Now, look here. If you go on talking to me like this I shall get quite cross. I'm doing my best to keep my temper as it is.
ELLEN	(*contemptuous*) Your temper! You can't pull wool over my eyes, Albert! Now listen. You'll start tomorrow. I'm coming with you. Bates will be here directly after breakfast.
ALBERT	(*now thoroughly alarmed*) But I daren't go up to London! I might be recognised.
ELLEN	You're not going to London. Bates will drive us to Maidstone. Then we'll make our way

across country by coach to Southampton.
There's a boat leaving for Quebec on Friday.
I've got your ticket. I've got everything.

ALBERT   (*grumbling*) You're going to a great deal of
trouble to get rid of me.

ELLEN   It isn't easy to pass on bad coins.

ALBERT   By Jove, you are a hard woman, Auntie.

ELLEN   Perhaps I am. Perhaps circumstances have
made me so. And you haven't helped to make
me any softer.

ALBERT   I don't know why you're suddenly so down on me.

ELLEN   (*quietly, but with great bitterness*) I've got to
know you better. I've watched you very
carefully the last few days. You're not a bit
sorry for what you've done. You haven't
shown a spark of gratitude to me. You're
thoroughly callous. You've demoralised your
aunts. Goodness knows what harm you've
done to that young girl. You've nosed about
the house and spied on everybody. If I hadn't
put my cash box in a very secure place I'm
quite sure your light fingers would have found
a way to it. And I'm saying this to my sister's son!

ALBERT   (*half whimpering*) You are full of the milk of
human kindness, aren't you? I suppose you
realise I've never had a chance - brought up
as I was. It's not my fault if I'm ambitious.

ELLEN   (*scornfully*) Ambitious!

ALBERT   Yes. Ambitious. I don't want to be downed all
my life - with other people's footmarks all
over me. I want to be on top. And I'm going
to be!

ELLEN   Well, you're not going to climb there on my
shoulders! I've made up my mind, and it's no
use arguing with me. You're going out of this
house before you're a day older.

ALBERT (*plucking up his courage*) I see. That's what you think. Does it occur to you that I may not go?

ELLEN Well, I can't throw you out physically, but I can always send for the police.

ALBERT Somehow I'd got the impression you didn't want the police here.

ELLEN Does that mean you refuse to go?

ALBERT Well, I certainly shan't go tomorrow morning.

(*He sits on the settle with his pipe between his lips.*)

ELLEN I'm afraid you'll have to.

ALBERT No. On second thoughts I'm quite content to stay for the time being. I'm getting fond of the place. The air suits me. You can't bluff me, you know.

ELLEN (*angrily*) I'm not bluffing you, Albert. I'm ordering you to go.

ALBERT Order, my foot! I'll tell you what I think of your reasons for wanting me out of the house. Bunkum.

ELLEN What do you mean?

ALBERT There's another you haven't mentioned, isn't there? A sounder one.

ELLEN (*facing up to the issue*) Yes. There is.

ALBERT Ah, now we're getting down to brass tacks. It's about Miss Fiske, isn't it?

ELLEN Yes, it is. (*Quite naturally.*) I met her in town today. She's coming back.

ALBERT (*absolutely staggered*) You met her in town, you say?

ELLEN   Yes. Why shouldn't I?

ALBERT   (*nonplussed*) No reason.

ELLEN   (*watching him closely*) I had to take her some
                 money that came for her.

ALBERT   I'd got it into my head that she'd gone for good.

ELLEN   Who gave you that idea? It's her house.
                 There's never been any question of her not
                 coming back.

ALBERT   Well, in that case, why spend the last half
                 hour abusing me? Why not tell me straight
                 away I'd got to go because she was coming back?

ELLEN   I didn't want you to know anything about it.

ALBERT   Why not?

ELLEN   You're such a chatterbox. You'd go blurting it
                 out to your aunts. And it would be fatal if
                 they got to know about it now. Because -
                 don't you see? It means that they've got to
                 go, too. They'll be dreadfully upset about it.
                 You know what they are. And I shall have to
                 break it to them very gently.

ALBERT   (*almost convinced*) Oh, well — there's
                 nothing for it, then. My little country holiday
                 has obviously come to an end. I'll have to
                 thank you for your loving care, Auntie, and
                 kiss you good bye. I don't know what the
                 blazes I'll do in Canada. But I suppose one
                 can starve there as well as anywhere else.

ELLEN   I shall give you something to start on. I can't
                 do less, for Rose's sake. I've no doubt you'll
                 pick up a living somehow.

ALBERT   I'll do my best to deserve your good opinion,
                 Auntie. And I suppose I ought to be grateful.

ELLEN   I'm not asking for that.

ALBERT   Well, I'd better get some sleep, hadn't I? I'm
                going to have a tiring day tomorrow.

                (*He has risen. A sudden thought strikes him,
                and, while closely watching her, he knocks his
                pipe on the bake-oven door. The tap-tap of the
                wood on the metal sounds extraordinarily
                sinister. It is as if somebody inside were
                knocking.* ELLEN *rises with a little shudder.*
                ALBERT *comes forward.*)

ALBERT   Do we kiss good night?

ELLEN   No.

ALBERT   (*looking into her drawn face*) I say! You're
                looking rather played out. Hadn't you better
                toddle off, too?

ELLEN   (*with an effort*) I'm just coming. I've got to
                lock up.

                (*She locks the front door.* ALBERT *goes to the
                stairway. Then he turns.*)

ALBERT   Oh, I forgot to tell you. I had a funny dream
                last night, Auntie.

ELLEN   (*turning to him*) What was that?

ALBERT   I dreamt Miss Fiske was dead.

ELLEN   (*facing him coolly*) Oh?

                (*He goes upstairs.* ELLEN *stands alone, her
                face working. Then she crosses and kneels for
                a moment on the prie dieu in an attitude of
                agonized supplication. It is indeed the
                revelation of a soul in torment. She is shaken
                with half-suppressed sobs. After a moment she
                rises from her knees, turns out one lamp and
                takes up the other, and then goes upstairs
                leaving the stairway door open behind her.
                The only light in the room is the dim glow of
                the fire. The grandfather clock strikes eleven.
                Then* ALBERT *appears coming softly down the*

*stairs in his stockinged feet with a lighted
candle. He goes to the hearth, and fiddles
with the bake-oven door, though it's hard to
see what he's doing. Then he leaves it, tiptoes
to the kitchen door which he opens and
whistles softly. He comes to the piano, sits at
it and plays the "Tit-Willow" tune. As he
finishes he hears something, and, rising from
the piano, slips into the kitchen.* ELLEN
*appears on the stairs carrying a lighted night
light in a victorian night light holder. She
comes into the room, holding it up. Her face
is haggard.)*

ELLEN

Albert! Was that you?

*(There is no answer. She goes to the hearth
and shines her light on the bake-oven door. It
is open and the bricked-up wall is showing.
This discovery has quite an effect upon her.
She crosses the room to the front door, throws
it open and the moonlight streams in. She
turns towards the piano and there, as the
moonlight falls across the room, she sees the
figure of* LEONORA FISKE *seated at the keys.
Her head is bent, but her auburn wig, her
violet dress and green shawl are
unmistakable. The figure makes a deliberate
movement and, as it rises,* ELLEN *gives a
gasping cry of "Leonora" and falls to the
ground in a faint of fit. Almost immediately*
ALBERT *enters from the kitchen. He carries his
candle and, in the brighter light, you see that
the figure of* LEONORA *is in reality* LUCY
*dressed in her clothes, who has slipped in
unperceived while* ELLEN *was at the hearth.*
LUCY *advances tremblingly to the prostate*
ELLEN.)*

LUCY

Albert! She's fainted What have you made me
do?

(Blackout.)

Scene Two

It is nine o'clock the next morning, a clear, sunny day. The room is empty. The bake-oven door is shut. As the lights rise the clock is striking. A knocking at the front door breaks into this, and LUCY *crosses the room from the kitchen to open it. She goes out into the porch.*

LUCY   Good morning, Mr Bates. Oh, are you ordered?

BATES' VOICE Miss Creed ordered me. It's for Maidstone.

LUCY   I don't think she's very well this morning, but I'll see.

              (*She returns to the room, half closing the door.* ALBERT *enters from the kitchen, his napkin to his mouth.*)

ALBERT   Who is it?

LUCY   It's Bates. He says he's got to go to Maidstone.

ALBERT   Oh, no, he hasn't. Tell him the order's cancelled.

LUCY   But, Albert . . .

ALBERT   Do what I tell you.

              (*He stands listening.* LUCY *returns to the porch.*)

LUCY   (*off*) Miss Creed's very sorry, Mr Bates, but she won't be wanting you this morning after all. She's poorly.

BATES   (*off*) Nothing serious, I hope?

LUCY   (*off*) Oh, no, nothing serious.

BATES   (*off*) Then I'll be gettin' along. Between you and me I'm not sorry. I've gotter go kill a pig.

LUCY   (*off*) Good morning.

              (*She returns as the cart moves away.*)

ALBERT   (*with a jerk of his thumb toward upstairs*) No
                  sign of her yet?

LUCY   No. She did look ill when I took in her early
                  tea. Albert, I'm scared. I wish I knew if she
                  thought it was me dressed up.

ALBERT   Of course she didn't. She doesn't know it was
                  you any more than the man in the moon. She
                  thinks she saw a ghost.

LUCY   All the same, I can t help wishing we hadn't
                  done it - now. I never thought she'd take it so
                  badly and go and faint. She might have died.
                  Then we'd have been responsible.

ALBERT   You pull yourself together. She didn't die.
                  She's very much alive. And we proved what
                  we wanted, didn't we?

LUCY   Yes. I suppose we did.

ALBERT   We've proved that Miss Fiske's dead, and she
                  knows it.

LUCY   But what puzzles me is how could Miss Fiske
                  die and she be the only one to know it?

ALBERT   (*cunningly*) Don't you see? Miss Fiske may
                  have died on her holiday - in some lonely
                  place? And Aunt Ellen may have had her
                  buried and said nothing about it?

LUCY   (*struck*) I see . . .

ALBERT   And don't you see - that gives us a strong
                  pull? If I'm right, she'll have to cough up
                  what we want.

LUCY   I can't go on with it. It frightens me.

ALBERT   You haven't got to. You've only got to help
                  me. I'm doing it all. And, when we've lined
                  our pockets, we'll take a little trip and have a

look at the world. We two, eh? Like that, won't you?

LUCY   I shall have it on my conscience for the rest of my life.

(LOUISA *enters from the kitchen.*)

LOUISA   Albert, your tea's getting cold, dear. What have you been doing?

ALBERT   Lucy and I've been having a chat to old Bates. He's been telling us all the news of the outside world.

LOUISA   (*eagerly*) Oh, Albert, do tell me!

ALBERT   It'll tickle you to death. Weeping whiskers are coming in again.

(LUCY *goes into the kitchen.*)

LOUISA   (*laughing*) Oh, Albert! Get along with you! You're never serious. I don't know whether we ought to be laughing -with Ellen so ill upstairs.

ALBERT   Of course you oughtn't. You're very wicked, Aunt Louisa.

(EMILY *enters from the kitchen. She carries a plate of stale bread. She puts this on the piano and stands there crumbling it.*)

EMILY   Aren't you going to finish your breakfast, Albert?

ALBERT   No, I've had enough. I'm a bit off this morning.

EMILY   That means it'll be wasted. You shouldn't have kept him. Louisa.

ALBERT   Don't blame the old bell of Bow, Aunt Emily. (*To* LOUISA.) It's not your fault if you're so fetching, is it, my puss?

LOUISA   Isn't he ridiculous, Emily?

EMILY	He's making a fool of you, Louisa. He's making a fool of all of us. I believe he could make a fool of Ellen if he tried.
ALBERT	A fool of Aunt Ellen, Aunt Emily? Oh, no. It would take someone much cleverer than me to do that. (*At the stairs.*) Well, I'm going upstairs to cut my throat.

(*He goes.* LOUISA *follows him to the foot of the stairs.*)

LOUISA	What did you say, Albert? (*To* EMILY, *in distress.*) Oh, what does he mean, Emily?
EMILY	(*crumbling her bread*) You're so simple, Louisa. He's going to shave. He thought he was being funny. Stupid boy.
LOUISA	Why are you always so against everybody, Emily?
EMILY	I'm not against everybody.
LOUISA	Yes, you are. You're against Albert. You'd be against Ellen, if you dared. I expect you're against me - only you don't say so.
EMILY	I don't take all that much notice of you.
LOUISA	(*mysteriously*) I know something about you. I know you were frightened about Ellen last night. I've never seen anyone so frightened.
EMILY	Everybody was frightened.
LOUISA	What do you think was the matter with her? Why did she faint like that? It wasn't like Ellen. Ellen doesn't faint.
EMILY	I think she was walking in her sleep. I've heard her go downstairs on other nights. I think her thoughts of Miss Fiske are at the back of it.

LOUISA	(*nodding*) Yes, Miss Fiske. She's behind everything in this house, isn't she? I've always hated her.
EMILY	Perhaps she hates us.
LOUISA	Do you know, Emily, I'm sometimes so afraid that Miss Fiske will get the better of Ellen? I sometimes think she wants to come back and turn us out.
EMILY	I don't think she ever sold the house to Ellen. I think Ellen's deceiving us. I think Miss Fiske's here now.
LOUISA	Oh, Emily, you frighten me! Why do you say that?
EMILY	Didn't you hear it?
LOUISA	Hear what?
EMILY	The piano - last night. That was Miss Fiske's music. Her silly tune. Tit-Willow, Tit-Willow.
LOUISA	You heard it, too? I heard it. I thought it was in a dream. In my head.
	(ELLEN *comes downstairs. She looks wan and ill. But her intense agony of mind gives her a certain fineness, almost a greatness. She carries her cloak and bonnet and a reticule.*)
ELLEN	What are you two whispering about?
LOUISA	Oh, Ellen! You've come down! Do you think you're well enough?
ELLEN	It's all right, darling. I'm quite strong again.
EMILY	You'd better have the doctor.
ELLEN	A doctor couldn't do any good. It's nothing.
LOUISA	But, Ellen, you walked in your sleep last night.
ELLEN	I wasn't asleep, Louisa. I wasn't even undressed. I knew what I was doing. I thought I heard someone moving about the house.

EMILY	But then, if you were wide awake, Ellen, why did you scream?
ELLEN	I thought I saw someone. But it turned out to be nobody.
LOUISA	It's funny you should have thought you saw someone. Because Emily and I thought we heard someone.
ELLEN	Who do you think you heard?
EMILY	Miss Fiske.
LOUISA	We thought we heard her at the piano. She was playing that sad little song about the willow tree. You remember how she was always playing it?
ELLEN	I remember.
EMILY	I thought it might have been Albert up to one of his tricks. But he was upstairs all the time. Because I heard him come up and go into his room before you.
LOUISA	It is strange, isn't it, Ellen?
ELLEN	(*wearily*) There's no point in going on talking about it.
LOUISA	Oh, Ellen! I've got an idea! Such a dreadful idea, Ellen! What if Miss Fiske should be hiding somewhere in the house! And she's playing tricks on us to punish us for being here!
ELLEN	Don't talk so foolishly, darling. Miss Fiske's a long way away.
EMILY	You'd better let me sleep in your room tonight, Ellen. In case you wake in your sleep again.
ELLEN	I've told you I wasn't asleep.

EMILY   But you often walk about in the night, Ellen. Perhaps you don't know it, but you do. People don't know it when they walk in their sleep.

ELLEN   I've been a little worried since Albert's been here. He's so unreliable. Why, he might take it into his head to go for a walk in the middle of the night and leave the door open! You never know what he may do.

EMILY   But you started walking about in the night long before Albert came, Ellen.

ELLEN   Oh, no, I didn't, Emily. You know you never remember things right.

EMILY   (*resentfully*) Very well.

               (*She takes up her plate of crumbled bread.*)

LOUISA   Where are you going?

EMILY   I'm going down to the Priory to feed the jackdaws. I put out my crusts along the top of the wall and they come down from the tower and take them.

LOUISA   Oh, I should like to see them, Emily!

EMILY   They won't come if you're there. You're all chatter, chatter, chatter.

LOUISA   Oh, Emily.

ELLEN   Take her with you please, Emily. (*She is now on the sofa.*) I'd like to sit here alone.

EMILY   Well, you'll have to keep very quiet. Do you understand?

LOUISA   Yes, Emily. I'll be as still as a statue, I won't move or speak at all. And, oh, Emily, I think I'll take my telescope and I'll watch the ships while you're waiting for your jackdaws and I can describe them to you.

EMILY   (*going out of the front door*) Chatter, chatter, chatter.

               (LOUISA *follows her, carrying her telescope, and the front doors shuts.* LUCY *enters.*)

LUCY   Oh, are you down, Miss? Are you better?

ELLEN   (*lying back on the sofa*) Yes, thank you, Lucy.

LUCY   I'm so glad. Can I get you a cup of tea or anything?

ELLEN   No. I've got to go out in a minute. Bates ought to be here now. Go and see if there's any sign of him.

LUCY   Bates? But he's been and gone, Miss!

ELLEN   Been and gone?

LUCY   Yes, Miss. Mr Albert sent him away. He thought you were too poorly to get up.

ELLEN   Where is Mr Albert?

LUCY   I don't know where he's gone, Miss. He's had his breakfast.

ELLEN   Try and find him, and tell him I want him.

LUCY   Yes, Miss.

               (*She goes upstairs.* ELLEN *rises, crosses to the hearth and peers at the closed door of the bake-oven.*)

ELLEN   . . . Imagination . . .

               (*She returns to the sofa and lies down.* ALBERT *comes softly downstairs. He is carrying a wig block on which is* LEONORA'S *auburn wig, but he conceals it from* ELLEN *by keeping it on the far side of him. He closes the door very gently and, coming forward, places the wig block on the piano. Then he stands between it and his aunt. She does not realise he is there till he speaks.*)

ALBERT   (*cheerily*) Good morning, Aunt Ellen. We
                didn't expect you down today.

ELLEN   Well, you were wrong. Is that why you sent
                Bates away?

ALBERT   Partly.

ELLEN   What do you mean by interfering with my
                arrangements? When you said goodnight to
                me last night you'd quite excepted the idea of
                going to Canada.

ALBERT   You're forgetting, Auntie. That was the *first*
                time we said goodnight. When we said
                goodnight a second time you weren't in any
                shape to be jolted to Maidstone in the
                morning.

ELLEN   That was nothing. Only a little faintness.
                Well, you'll have to get hold of Bates
                somehow. We'll go tomorrow instead. You're
                going to catch that boat. You understand that?

ALBERT   I hear what you say.

ELLEN   They tell me you were very good to me last
                night. I'd like to say thank you.

ALBERT   Oh, that was only nephewly feeling. Besides,
                we must take care of the goose that lays the
                golden eggs, mustn't we?

ELLEN   What d'you mean?

ALBERT   Well, that's what you are, aren't you? You're
                very valuable to all of us.

ELLEN   (*bitterly*) I suppose I am. I've always had to
                provide. That's been my life - in one word.
                Provide.

ALBERT   It was a strange turn you had. What actually
                happened?

ELLEN   I don't know. I must have had some kind of
                 nervous seizure.

ALBERT   Yes, I'd noticed you seemed a bit nervy.

ELLEN   It's because I haven't been sleeping.

ALBERT   That's a thing I can't understand, you know.
                 Not sleeping. I sleep like a top. I expect
                 you'd say that's because I haven't got a
                 conscience to worry me!

ELLEN   Do you imagine my not sleeping has anything
                 to do with conscience?

ALBERT   (*cocking his head to one side*) Hasn't it?

ELLEN   What's behind that remark, Albert?

ALBERT   Nothing. (*With a change of tone.*) Auntie, I've
                 got a little confession to make.

ELLEN   (*startled*) What! Another!

ALBERT   Yes. I've deceived you. It's been on my mind
                 for some time, but I've kept forgetting.

ELLEN   (*watching him closely*) What is it?

ALBERT   Don't get cross, will you? You were away last
                 June fetching your sisters, weren't you? Well,
                 I called here. And I met Miss Fiske.

ELLEN   (*her eyes never leaving him*) Oh?

ALBERT   Yes. She was very kind to me. I quite took to
                 her. I was a bit short at the time and she lent
                 me some ready. Out of her little safe there,
                 you know. The one that's bricked up now. We
                 agreed not to tell you. We thought it might
                 worry you. But now I think you ought to
                 know. (*Taking out his pipe.*) Do you mind if I
                 smoke, or would it upset you?

                 (*He strolls to the far side of the piano,
                 disclosing, by doing so, the wig on the wig*)

block. ELLEN *stares at it. There is a pause. It is as though the missing woman had suddenly come into the room.* ELLEN *rises, still staring at it.* ALBERT *watches her cunningly.)*

ELLEN (*with a sort of slow horror*) You know?

ALBERT (*lightly*) Aha.

ELLEN It was you last night, too.

ALBERT (*nodding, laconically*) Me and Lucy.

ELLEN Lucy?

ALBERT It's all right. I took care she didn't know what I know.

ELLEN And I gave you sanctuary!

ALBERT (*shrewdly*) It wasn't yours to give, was it?

ELLEN (*bracing herself to seem almost casual*) Well, now you know - what are you going to do?

ALBERT Do? Nothing. You've told me nothing. I know nothing.

ELLEN But you - you want something?

ALBERT Oh. yes. I want something. You know, Auntie, I always had a fancy to settle in the country.

ELLEN You don't mean - here?

ALBERT Why not? I could help you keep an eye on - things. I shan't lose my nerve. Oh, and I shall want a little wedding present. I may have to marry Lucy. We shall be a very happy little family here, shan't we? How long do you think it'll last?

ELLEN How long will what last?

ALBERT Her money.

ELLEN I see. So you've come to the conclusion that it's safer to be a receiver than a thief?

ALBERT   They're both safer than being a - but don't
                 let's call each other names, Auntie. That
                 won't get us anywhere.

ELLEN   Is there anything else you'd like?

ALBERT   No. That'll do to go on with.

ELLEN   Then I think it's about time you went out and
                 ordered Bates - at once.

ALBERT   You're a cool one, aren't you? Barring little
                 incidents like last night of course. I take off
                 my hat to you.

ELLEN   I think you're rather brave, too, Albert.

ALBERT   Oh, no, not brave Auntie. Just cunning.

ELLEN   You surely don't propose to go on living here
                 - with me?

ALBERT   Why not?

ELLEN   (*with superb irony*) Well, for one thing, you'd
                 never be quite sure, would you? There are
                 more ways than one, you know.

ALBERT   (*in amazement*) You wouldn't dare, a second time.

ELLEN   What makes you so sure?

ALBERT   (*daunted in spite of himself*) Supposing I said
                 I'd risk it?

ELLEN   You won't. Now that I've frightened you.
                 You've got a very good appetite, haven't you,
                 Albert? And you'd hardly be likely to enjoy
                 your meals.

ALBERT   Easy on, Aunt. I can see through you. You're
                 bluffing.

ELLEN   Am I? D'you think I'm going to let a little
                 thing like you stand in my way? It takes a lot
                 of courage to kill for the first time. (*In a*

whisper.) But once you've sold your soul to the Devil it comes easier. (*There is a pause. He watches her, fascinated.*) I think you know why I did - what I did. I did it to secure to my poor sisters a little of what the world owes them. They're all I have. They're my children. They were left in my care. I think you know what I've suffered. You've seen me in torment. You've helped to torture me. But don't think I'm going to hand over what I've taken to a little whippersnapper who's repaid my kindness with cheap treachery.

ALBERT   (*thinking better of it*) Very good. What's it worth to you if I do order Bates and clear out? When all's said, we're both after the same thing - cash - aren't we?

ELLEN   I told you last night what I'll give you.

ALBERT   I'll take five hundred. And the old girl's earrings for Lucy.

ELLEN   No.

ALBERT   Well, forget the earrings, then.

ELLEN   You're wasting your breath.

ALBERT   You wouldn't like me to suggest to the police that they came and did a bit of renovating to your chimney piece, would you?

ELLEN   I don't quite see you going to the police.

ALBERT   Oh, they'd forget what I've done if I went and told 'em . . . (*He is back at the piano and fondles* LEONORA's *false curls.*) . . . that the head that wore this hasn't any more use for a wig.

ELLEN   No, Albert - you've chosen the wrong moment. It's broad daylight - now.

(*There is a sudden quick rapping at the door. Both are electrified for a moment. Then* ALBERT *snatches the antimacassar from the*

sofa and adroitly flings it over the wig block.
ELLEN *opens the door.* SISTER THERESA *enters.*)

THERESA — Oh, I'm sorry if I'm interrupting, but I wanted to see you, Miss Creed, if I could. And I particularly didn't want to disturb the others.

ELLEN — Yes, Sister? Good morning. What can I do?

THERESA — (*as she sees* ALBERT) I'm glad your nephew's here. It's really no business of mine and I oughtn't to have come. But we've just had a call at the Priory - from the police. They've driven over from Gravesend.

ALBERT — (*alert and alarmed*) Gravesend?

THERESA — (*significantly*) Yes. I heard them talking to the Reverend Mother. They're looking for a young man who's supposed to have taken money from a bank. He's been traced to the marshes. They gave a very complete description of him, and it tallied so closely with your nephew that I thought I'd come and let you know. Of course, if I knew it was your nephew it would be very wrong of me to warn you.

ALBERT — Did the Reverend Mother say I was here?

THERESA — She doesn't know. I'm the only one at the Priory who does. She told them that, at the moment there were simply three elderly ladies living at Estuary House. And, of course, so far as she knew, that was the truth. So the officers have gone down to the marsh - to Decoy Farm. But I thought I ought to come up and tell you because Miss Fiske's such a great mutual friend. I know she would like me to.

ALBERT — Well, on her behalf, old lady, thanks for the tip.

THERESA — It was you? I was afraid so. I'm so sorry.

ALBERT	So am I. But we can't go into that now. I've got to look slippy. Got any cash handy, Auntie?
ELLEN	Yes. (*She gives him her reticule.*) You can take this. It hasn't what you wanted in it, but it's not empty.
ALBERT	Oh - thanks. If I write you can send on the rest. So long, Sister. No hard feelings, Aunt. (*Significantly.*) And remember - there's nothing to worry about. This sees you right.
ELLEN	You'll find your ticket in there, too.
ALBERT	Good! I'll get that boat somehow. I'd better slip out the back way and through the woods. (*As an afterthought.*) Er - tell Lucy.
	(*He goes.*)
THERESA	I had a brother rather like that. They're so easily lost, aren't they?
ELLEN	Albert was born without a conscience. That's all.
THERESA	It's very sad. Perhaps this will be a lesson to him. I hope he gets away. I'm afraid that's why I came. Was it very wrong of me?
ELLEN	I'm not a very good judge of what's right or wrong, but I'm afraid, in Albert's case, it's only postponing the evil day.
THERESA	Oh, well, you know - postponement's life.
ELLEN	Is it? Yes, I suppose, in the case of the little sinner, it is. But if one has sinned *very* deeply, postponement can be death. It can be worse than death.
THERESA	Oh? I suppose you're talking of what they call the Death-in-Life?

ELLEN   Do they call it that?

THERESA But it doesn't apply to your nephew. He's
         young. He may change. I suppose I'm rather
         simple minded. We're always praying to be
         delivered from evil. And I find it so difficult
         to believe that it exists. I suppose that's why
         I've never got any higher in my order. I
         haven't enough faith. You'll please not tell
         anyone I came, will you? ~~move behind E &~~
         door, try

ELLEN   Thank you for coming. Thank you for warning us.

         exit (THERESA *goes.* ELLEN *goes into the kitchen
         calling "Lucy, Lucy!"* LUCY *enters from the
         stairway door. Her face is white and horror-
         struck. You realise at once that she has been
         following* ALBERT'S *advice and listening. She
         makes for the front door.* ELLEN *returns from
         the kitchen.*)

         Lucy! Where are you going?

         (LUCY *turns but she cannot answer. She stands
         facing her mistress.*)

         Come here. I've something to tell you. (*There
         is a pause.* LUCY *does not move.*) It's about
         Mr Albert. (*Still* LUCY *does not answer. Then*
         ELLEN *speaks in a vibrant tone.*) Have you
         been listening?

         (*She steps towards her. Then* LUCY *screams. it
         is a wild terrified scream. She recovers the
         power of movement and turns and rushes out
         of the front door.* ELLEN *follows.*)

         (*calling*) Lucy! Lucy!

         (*But* LUCY *has gone like the wind.* ELLEN
         *comes back into the room. She has her hand
         to her heart. She leans on the back of the sofa
         for support.*)

         (*in a whisper*) The Death-in-Life.

(With an effort, she begins, very deliberately, to put on her cloak and bonnet. LOUISA *and* EMILY *enter by the front door.)*

LOUISA   It's quite warm out. Ellen. You wouldn't think it was November. We fed the jackdaws. But they wouldn't come down on the wall till we went away.

EMILY   *(she has a little bunch of black feathers in her hand)* That's because Louisa would chatter.

LOUISA   *(placing her telescope back on the dresser)* I was telling her about the ships. *(Noticing* ELLEN's *bonnet.)* Why, Ellen, where are you going?

ELLEN   Out.

LOUISA   Oh! As we were coming up the lane we met Lucy. She was running so fast. We thought there was something the matter. We really thought she must be coming to fetch us. But she climbed over the stile and ran down the path towards that farm on the marsh. *(Coming to the table where* EMILY *is toying with the feathers.)* What's it called, Emily?

EMILY   I told you — Decoy Farm.

ELLEN   *(putting on her cloak)* Decoy Farm. That's right. That's where I'm going.

LOUISA   Why are you going there, Ellen?

ELLEN   There are some gentlemen there — from Gravesend. I want to see them.

LOUISA   Gravesend? Oh, are they friends of Albert's?

ELLEN   No, darling. Nothing to do with Albert. It's a personal matter.

LOUISA   You won't bring them here, will you, Ellen?
              It's so nice and peaceful by ourselves.

ELLEN   No. I'll try not to bring them here. (*She
              stands watching the two old simpletons
              playing with their feathers. It is rather
              moving.*) You *have* been happy here, haven't
              you?

LOUISA   We are happy, Ellen. Aren't we, Emily?

EMILY   It's much better than London, certainly.

LOUISA   And it's so good of you to have bought this
              house for us! (*Looking up gratefully.*) You
              have been clever!

              (ELLEN *moves to the front door.*)

LOUISA   How long will you be?

ELLEN   I don't know, darling. I may be quite a time.
              (*She is standing in the sunlight and says with
              a sudden smile*). Oh, it's a lovely day!

LOUISA   We can look after ourselves. Can't we, Emily?

EMILY   Yes. We can look after ourselves.

              (ELLEN *goes out of the house. The two old
              ladies, happily occupied in themselves, are at
              the table fingering the black feathers. There
              is a short pause, and the lights fade.*)

PROPERTY LIST

ACT ONE
Scene One

On Stage: Piano
                on piano: Leather bound music score
                              Silver snuff box
                              Silver sweet box with sweets
                              Chinese Mandarin
            Bible on altar
            Statue of Madonna and Child
            Two altar candles
            Cash box with bag of sovereigns in bake oven
            "Slice" for bake oven in hearth
            Two oil lamps (unlit)
            Letters and envelopes in bureau

Off Stage: Vase of kingcups (LEONORA)
            Parcel containing score of "Mikado" (LUCY)
            Travelling bag (LUCY)
            Brace of curlew (LUCY)

ACT ONE
Scene Two

On Stage: Nautical Telescope
            Workbag
            Shawl
            Desert plate, knife and fork

Off Stage: Bottle of furniture polish and duster (ELLEN)
            Basket of pears (LEONORA)
            Driftwood (EMILY)
            Seaweed (EMILY)
            Tern (EMILY)
            Shells (EMILY)
            Dead bird (EMILY)
            Dustpan and brush (LUCY)

ACT ONE
Scene Three

Off Stage: Tin trunk (LEONORA *and* ELLEN)
Ladies elastic-sided boots (ELLEN)
Nautical telescope (LEONORA)
Strand of "Traveller's Joy" (EMILY)
Boots (EMILY)
Two turves of peat (LEONORA)
Bottle of champagne, glass (LEONORA)
Pink dressing gown and cord (ELLEN)

ACT TWO
Scene One

On Stage: Two wine glasses on dresser
Two egg cups on dresser
Bars over windows
Brick backing for oven
Taper (unlit) in hearth
Devotional book on table

Off Stage: Storm lantern, umbrella (SISTER THERESA)
Can of oil (LOUISA)
Tray with box of shells, pot of glue, etc. (EMILY)
Two umbrellas (LUCY)
Dressing gown (LOUISA)
Dark lantern (ALBERT)
Tray with meat, cognac, grapes, etc. (ELLEN)
Rug (LUCY)
Skeleton keys, wax vestas, cigar (ALBERT)

ACT TWO
Scene Two

On Stage: Gong
Quill pen, envelopes, letter paper on bureau
"Slice" for bake oven in hearth
"Mikado" and "Elijah" scores on piano

Off Stage: Bank letter with cheque, to be delivered
               Letter (SISTER THERESA)
               Mirror (LUCY)
               Wire and pliers (LUCY)
               Tray of sea shells, etc. (EMILY)
               Boiling kettle (LUCY)
               Spray of bryony berries (EMILY)
               Can of oil (SISTER THERESA)
               Razor, shaving brush, towel and soap (ALBERT)

ACT THREE
Scene One

On Stage: Square of green baize to cover table
               Cribbage board and pegs, cards, coins
               Bottle of cognac and glass on dresser
               EMILY'S tray of sea shells, etc.

Off Stage: Tray with milk and sandwiches (LUCY)
               Candle (ALBERT)
               Night light in holder (ELLEN)
               Pipe, skeleton keys (Albert)
               Crochet (LOUISA)

ACT THREE
Scene Two

On Stage: Nautical telescope
               Antimacassar

Off Stage: Napkin (ALBERT)
               Plate with crusts of bread (EMILY)
               Cloak and bonnet (ELLEN)
               LEONORA'S wig on block (Albert)
               Black feathers (EMILY *and* LOUISA)
               Pipe, etc. (ALBERT)

4pm next Sunday

! piece for the programme
  (get it done fast!)

Need to think about
   characters - jolly etc
! make her a person

She is jolly, happy
   content but savvy too
   more theatrical

calmness of a nun - stillness

sun
x Next Friday in Theatre.

Carol
07780860436.

Sunday 18

2pm + 6pm

tech   runs

10th Photos Sat 10pm

Next Friday – curry
       after reh

6:30 – 7

01926 863334
2 - 8PM

Prime of Miss Jean Brodie
Crucible
Animal Farm

Fri 30th
Ken Weekly News
Review.